Walking Nantucket

A Walkers Guide to Exploring Nantucket on Foot

Faraway Publishing Group

Copyright © 2021 All photos, drawings, and maps courtesy of Faraway Publishing Group. Illustrations and maps by Rose Gonnella. Photos by Rob Benchley and Michael Galvin. All rights reserved. Text copyright © 2003 by Peter B. Brace. Printed in the United States of America. No part of this book may be reproduced or transmitted in any form or by any means, electronic or mechanical, including photocopying, recording, of by an information storage and retrieval system, without written permission from the publisher.

ISBN 978-0-9720457-1-1

Published by Faraway Publishing Group, P.O. Box 792, Nantucket, MA 02554

Second Edition

Cover and interior designed by [work], workdesignlab.com
Printed by Studley Press, Massachusetts

Walking Nantucket

A Walkers Guide to Exploring Nantucket on Foot

By Peter B. Brace

With Maps and Illustrations by Rose Gonnella

and Photographs by Rob Benchley and Michael Galvin

Table of Contents by Habitat

6 + **Dedication** –

7 + **Acknowledgements** –

27 + **Shorelines** –
29 + Capaum Pond
35 + Coskata Pond
43 + Eel Point-North Point
51 + Little Neck
57 + The Creeks
62 + Polpis Harbor Boat Landing
69 + Quidnet-Sesachacha
75 + Smith's Point

83 + **Moors and Meadows**–
85 + Bald Spot Behind My House (Radar Hill)
91 + Head of the Plains
97 + Madequecham Valley
103 + Pout Ponds
111 + Sanford Farm
125 + Tupancy Links

— Forests + *131*

    Lost Farm Sanctuary + *133*

    Masquetuck + *141*

    Quidnet Route from Polpis Road + *147*

— Swamps, Bogs and Ponds + *153*

  Squam Farm + *155*

  Squam Swamp + *163*

  Tom Nevers Pond + *169*

  Windswept Cranberry Bog + *175*

— Neighborhoods + *187*

Lily Pond-Grove Lane + *189*

Siasconset Bluff + *195*

Squam Pond + *201*

Steps Beach + *207*

— Glossary + *214*

— Appendix + *219*

    — Resources used in producing this book + *222*

For my parents

Walking Nantucket is dedicated to my parents, Lloyd and Ann, who cared enough to show their three children the wonders of the outdoors. On hikes in the White Mountains, Lake Champlain by homemade boat, a bike trip to coastal Nova Scotia, and exploring the islands of Penobscot Bay, my father ingrained in us a lasting appreciation for the outside world. And my mother added to those experiences with trips to Nantucket where we rode horses out in the moors in the early seventies, on summer vacations to the shores of Lake Sebago in Maine, day trips to Plum Island in Newburyport, and extended getaways to our cottage on Vinalhaven Island, Maine. Were it not for my parents' guidance, I probably wouldn't ever have bought hiking boots, a mountain bike, or a kayak.

I love you both with all my heart and am eternally grateful for your support in the making of this book and my growth as a writer.

Acknowledgements

In the five years it took to bring *Walking Nantucket* from idea to reality, a staggering number of people and groups helped me get it all together, many of whom may not even realize the impact they had on the writing of this book. My late grandmother, Helen R. Brace, had a stalwart belief in my writing abilities that gave me the confidence that I needed to complete this book.

This project wouldn't even have become a reality had not my newspaper editor and friend, Reema Sherry, asked for weekly feature ideas for the back section of the *Nantucket Beacon*. I'd also like to thank the last publisher of the *Nantucket Beacon*, Marianne Stanton, for permitting me to publish in *Walking Nantucket* loose versions of some of my walks from my "Walking the Walks" series that ran in *Nantucket Beacon* from October 1997 to June 1998.

When the *Nantucket Beacon* ceased publication in August of 1998, I was without employment but only halfway through writing *Walking Nantucket*. I want to thank Friedrich Jaeger, publisher of *Times of the Islands: Nantucket & Martha's Vineyard*, who employed me as his editor. Peter Meerbergen hired me green as beach grass and he, along with Chadd Meerbergen and Donald Meyers, patiently imparted to me some of the essential skills of carpentry and historic house restoration. A few of them actually sunk in. And later, my last carpentry boss, who chose anonymity over fame, along with Moe Dee, Anthony Tobin, and Brody Pickman enlightened me with their knowledge of new house construction and taught me the Zen of the

Shovel, making sure I had plenty of deck footings to dig. Thank you for your friendship, your knowledge and your endless patience.

Brandt Gould gave me a few shifts a week at the door of Cambridge Street Victuals, and Kate Stout, former editor and publisher of *Map & Legend*, threw some freelance stories my way and later helped edit this book.

I would like to thank Rob Benchley and Michael Galvin, who shot all of the extraordinary black and white photos for *Walking Nantucket*. And I can't forget my Magellan of a mapmaker and illustrator, Rose Gonnella (also the designer of this book with Cesar Rubin and Alejandro Medina), and the person who probably knows Nantucket's wild lands better than I do, naturalist Cheryl Creighton, for helping me get my flora, fauna, and geology straight. And the executive director of the Nantucket Conservation Foundation, Jim Lentowski, my friend and long-time source, was vital in helping me keep my walks on land open to the public. He also educated me on Lyme disease. To all of you, I offer my deepest thanks and appreciation for your help in the production of my first book.

My thanks goes to Nancy Martin of Faraway Publishing Group for believing in my idea that people, islanders and visitors alike, need to know where to walk on Nantucket. Editing honors go to Jennifer Ahlborn and Kate Stout. And to my woman on the inside: thank you, Mercedes Chacon, for your invaluable knowledge of Nancy's daily schedule and her whereabouts whenever I needed to find her.

When shackled to my Macintosh G3, four Scots in possession of inspiring musical talent helped keep my fingers nimble, my wrists supple, and my thoughts lucid and flowing easily onto my screen. Thank you, the late Stuart Adamson, Tony Butler, Mark Brzezicki, and Bruce Watson.

And thanks to Coca-Cola, Ben & Jerry, SOBE, Provisions, Nantucket Beach Wok, Nantucket Bagel Company, Wilderness Systems, & Kenwood.

Do not leave Nantucket without seeing some of it on foot!

Before motorized vehicles made getting to downtown Nantucket a relatively quick commute from the outlying villages of Siasconset, Wauwinet, Madaket, Polpis, Pocomo, Quidnet, Tom Nevers, and Surfside, Nantucketers moved about their island on horseback, in livestock-drawn wagons, by rail, and on foot. On foot... imagine what they experienced while walking downtown from just Monomoy or Crooked Lane: birds, amphibians, plants, and mammals many now rare and endangered. Dozens of farms and the sweeping vistas of rolling grasslands of the past are now thickets of scrub oak and pitch pine dotted with kettle hole ponds on what Nantucketers call the moors.

Did you know that roughly 45 percent of 30,000-acre Nantucket Island is preserved and open to the public forever? That fact alone might compel you to see as much of its moors, bogs, beaches, salt marshes, streets, dirt roads, dunes, estuaries, harbors, ponds, creeks, and mud flats as you can. Because your time on Nantucket may be short, a bus tour or an auto, scooter, or bike rental might seem your only recourse to see any of Nantucket's preserved and vast wild lands. But as you're whizzing around the island on your wheeled conveyance, you won't truly see the island as its founders first experienced it in 1659. Only your two feet can show you the wonders of Coskata Pond at low tide, the squat oak and beech trees of Masquetuck, and the swans on Hummock Pond.

Maybe you have run across an island place name like Shawkemo, Long Pond, or Masquetuck, and had no idea where it was or how to get there. Maybe a friend has taken you for a walk through the Nantucket Conservation Foundation's prize property, Sanford Farm, and you thought you'd seen a sizeable chunk of Nantucket's open land. While that particular tract encompasses most of the ecosystems that you'll see on the

island, such as swamps, ponds, upland meadows, forests, and coastal heathland, it barely scratches the surface of the thousands of acres to be explored on Nantucket. *Walking Nantucket* can guide you to a Nantucket you have never seen.

This book is loosely based on "Walking the Walks," a series I wrote while in the employ of the *Nantucket Beacon*, but contains more detailed historical and natural information, as well as general recommendations for exploring Nantucket on foot. Before choosing a walk, please read the following information, which is designed to improve your experience while walking Nantucket.

Tread Lightly

Your feet will, at times when you don't even realize it, tread on fragile soils, exposed root systems, rare and endangered plants, and vegetation that can't survive being stepped on more than once or twice. Three of the island's conservation groups—the public Nantucket Islands Land Bank, and its nonprofit counterparts, the Nantucket Conservation Foundation and the Trustees of Reservations—have rangers and property managers who do their best to educate visitors on the sensitivity of lands under their care.

But these rangers can't be on all of their acres all of the time. *You* have to be your own ranger of the land you're exploring. It is extraordinarily valuable land, and we are lucky to enjoy so much open space on such a small island. By caring for these properties, we can show our gratitude to those who have given and preserved these lands.

I can't stress enough the imperative need for walkers on these properties to stick to established trails, not to pick the fruit of island plants, not to destroy any of the plants and not to pick flowers or harass any of the animals you encounter in your travels, to leave behind the rocks and shells you find on the beach along with any archeological artifacts you may discover, and carrying your litter out with you.

Nantucket's land conservation organizations aren't required to allow public use of their properties. They have the same cares and concerns for their land as any private property owner. But because a majority of islanders and seasonal residents alike thought it vital to the character of Nantucket that we all be able to enjoy a walk through the moors or a day at the beach without paying a fee or encountering a "no trespassing" sign, the preserved open space on Nantucket is yours to explore and enjoy.

With that in mind, because these properties are owned by responsible private groups, they do have the right to close any of their properties to the public as they see fit, for safety or other reasons. Also, due to erosion on the beaches, you may eventually find some of these walks can't be completed as described because the ocean has eaten away part of a trail or made a bluff too steep to walk down. When you encounter these obstacles, please be guided by common sense and choose another walk.

I have great reverence for these organizations that welcome the public to enjoy their land, and I understand that they trust that the public *won't do the land harm*. Make this your modus operandi whenever you walk on conservation land, and you'll always find it open to you.

Walk or Cycle When You Can

All of the walks in this book can be found by bicycle, and some by simply walking, depending on where you are on the island. So, since the premise of *Walking Nantucket* is walking, I urge you to consider leaving your automobile at home. Not only will you see more of Nantucket while walking, cycling, or riding on the bus than you would while driving with your eyes fixed on the road ahead, but you'll also be cutting down on pollution of our air and congestion of our already crowded island roads.

In addition, most of the trailheads for these walks offer extremely limited parking—in many cases fewer than five or six spaces. A fair number of the walks run near private property, and most of the parking areas are surrounded by fragile vegetation. Thus, if you find no available spots in the parking area of a walk, do not attempt to park outside the parking area on land obviously not designated for parking, on private property, or on the street. Instead, choose another walk where there is sufficient parking.

The Nantucket Regional Transit Authority (NRTA)

During its operational season, roughly from the end of May through the end of September, the NRTA buses offer another option to avoid traffic and parking problems: almost all of the walks are reasonably accessible via a NRTA route. If you came to the island without a vehicle or bicycle and are planning to get around under your own steam, the other vital maps you should secure before exploring my walks are those in the NRTA's brochure. But remember that not all the walks in this book are within reasonable walking distance of the NRTA bus stops. Consequently, if you don't see a NRTA stop noted at the bottom of a walk, the distance you would have to walk from the bus stop to the start of the walk is unreasonable.

Available at the Visitor Services & Information Bureau at 25 Federal Street, at the Nantucket Island Chamber of Commerce at 48 Main Street, and on the individual buses, the NRTA brochure outlines bus departure sites, the various island routes, and fares. The NRTA operates seven shuttle bus routes around Nantucket.

You can reach the NRTA by phone at 508-228-7025 or online at *http://www.town.nantucket.ma.us/departments/nrta/getaroundack/shuttle.html*

The Maps

Our mapmaker and illustrator, Rose Gonnella, whose internal compass threw its spindle years ago, originally thought it would be fun if the walk maps were more like treasure maps. That way, we reasoned, she could get out of trying to find west-southwest on a compass and you could have more fun exploring these walks on your own. However, after following all the walks together several times, we decided that in the interest of preventing you from getting lost, we would design our maps using a Geographical Information Systems (GIS) map from the town that exercises just the right amount of hand-holding. We consulted the United States Geological Survey (USGS) map of Nantucket as well.

The maps are to scale and will guide you along each walk safely and accurately. Our directions include key lefts and rights, as well as roads and other landmarks along the way. The maps were specifically drawn to leave a lot to the imagination. We want you to use them to complete each walk successfully, but we also want the maps to tempt you down established paths not included therein. Because it was impossible, and not particularly desirable, to include the entire island in this book, we hope the maps, coupled with their respective walks, will serve as your guide to Nantucket's outdoors.

Another word of caution: The land open to the public on Nantucket is interspersed with private properties and with fragile dune, coastal plain, heathland, and wetland ecosystems. In addition to respecting any private property that you encounter, do not attempt to explore any of these ecosystems, because your presence can do them irreparable, and usually fatal damage.

Before you don your explorer's cap and march out into the bush, I strongly recommend that you do two things. Learn to use, and bring with you, a compass, especially if you're an experienced and intrepid explorer and wish to walk off the maps.

Also, to supplement the basic map of the island at the start of this book, you should have one or two of several available island maps when you embark on any of these walks. The aforementioned USGS map is sold at the Nantucket Ship Chandlery, Old South Wharf, for about $25. While pricey, this official topographical map does include elevation contours and, even though drawn in 1979, will give you a more realistic sense of Nantucket's lands. The best all-around map of Nantucket is "Nantucket Island: Detailed street and road map". Available in numerous island book and gift stores, this map provides detailed maps of downtown and the major villages of Nantucket on the reverse side of a map of the entire island. The Nantucket Conservation Foundation, the oldest land conservation group on the island, produces an annual map of its

properties, using the USGS map as a background. This map is available at the Foundation's offices at 118 Cliff Road. Also, the Nantucket Islands Land Bank, 22 Broad Street, offers a rough map of some of its more popular island holdings. Sources of maps that will help you reach the starts of the walks are plentiful: the Visitor Services & Information Bureau at 25 Federal Street gives out maps of the island, including several of the downtown area; the island's bike shops provide basic island road maps to those renting their bikes, scooters, and cars; and the NRTA buses, the Visitor Bureau, and the Chamber of Commerce are all stocked with maps of the NRTA routes.

About My Directions

In leading you down the many paths in this book, you'll notice that I alternate between compass directions and instructions to walk left, right, forward, and backward, and in some cases, combinations of both. In some of the directions, it was necessary only to tell you "right" or "left" without including a compass point because I didn't want you to stop at every turn to take a compass reading to be certain you're making the correct turn.

This book doesn't offer a course in orienteering, nor should you spend all your time looking down at a compass instead of taking in the scenery. So read the walk before you start, look at its map, then get out there and do it. You may wish, though, to bring the book with you for quick reference.

Walking Distances

Most of the walks in this book are completed easily in less than one hour and cover fairly even ground. However, older walkers and those with physical handicaps should use a walk's length, listed below its title, as a guide for personal limitations when choosing a walk. The walks vary from less than half a mile to more than six miles in length.

Walk Difficulty Ratings

Since Nantucket is relatively flat, with hills not much higher than 100 feet, the walking, in terms of ascents and descents, is fairly easy. But the length of some of these walks can make them more strenuous than might be suggested by a walk on level ground.

So, to give you an idea of what your legs are in for while exploring Nantucket's wilderness, I've rated the degree of physical difficulty of each walk on a scale of one to four, marked in stars below the title of each walk.

The ratings take into account the mileage and terrain you will encounter on each walk. One star means that the walk is approximately a mile in distance and that most of you could, regardless of physical condition, complete the walk. A walk with two stars may be one to two miles along relatively moderate terrain. Walks with three stars can be two to four miles or more in length and will definitely give you a workout. Finally, four-star walks are four to six miles long over relatively rugged ground.

The Seasons

When choosing a walk from this book, you should consider the season. While all of these walks can be appreciated at any time of the year, you'll enjoy them more when you plan for weather, wildlife, and other users of the land.

For instance, since the predominantly southwestern wind that caresses Nantucket in the summer can reach gale force blowing out of the northeast and east in the fall and winter, I tend during those seasons to avoid the more exposed walks, such as those on the shores and mud flats. Instead, I'll choose to walk through the island's relatively protected interior.

Walks through swampy, moist, and wet areas are also more enjoyable in fall and winter, because mosquitoes and other winged pests are dormant during these seasons. As noted below, you'll want to avoid most interior sections of the island during deer-hunting season. Apart from such safety precautions, dress appropriately and follow any of these routes any time of year so you can experience the terrain and wildlife during each season.

The Orange People

The time of year to avoid walking in the moors, open fields, and island forests is the deer-hunting season for bow and arrow, shotgun, and primitive firearm hunters. While the hunters are after strictly the venison and not people out for walks, the danger of so many fluorescent orange-clad hunters with shotguns roaming the island is still quite real. Before you go out on any of these walks, especially in the woods, moors, and bogs, you should know when the orange people are out.

The Massachusetts' deer hunting opens with bow and arrow hunting from around the middle of October through end of the third week of November. Shotgun hunters are out in force for the first two weeks of December, and those hunters cunning enough to wield primitive firearms (muzzleloaders) can hunt on Nantucket from the middle of December through Dec. 31. The Massachusetts Division of Fisheries & Wildlife does change its hunting seasons from year to year, depending on game populations and other factors. To learn the latest season dates, call the Division at 508-759-3406.

For local concerns, you can reach Nantucket's Environmental Police Officer through the Nantucket Police Department at 508-228-1212. If you do plan to walk during hunting season, wear at least one article of the bright neon-orange colored clothing. Talking loudly and making noise as you go will also alert hunters to your presence. And if you bring your dog, keep it leashed and wearing either an orange collar or a vest to keep it safe.

Dogs

While Nantucket has a leash law that requires dog owners to leash their dogs at all times outside of their homes, the spirit of this law is typically observed more than the letter of the law. Hence, you'll see dogs running free all over Nantucket. What you should worry about is the safety of your own dog and how it will affect others if it isn't leashed. While out walking, you're likely to encounter equestrians, mountain bikers, and people running and walking with their own dogs, as well as the wildlife that you came to see. If your dog isn't leashed, riders may fall off their horses or bikes, runners could be scared or bitten, your dog could fight with other dogs, and that shorebird you wanted to see during its nesting period will be nowhere in sight.

My recommendation is to leash your dog for these walks, unless it is so well trained as to obey your every command. You should also carry with you plastic bags to remove and dispose of your dog's waste.

Fishing and Shellfish Digging

Many of the walks in *Walking Nantucket* will take you along the shores of harbors, ponds, and the ocean and were written in part to show that there's more to these walks than a good stretch of the legs. To wit, the low tide jaunts are perfect for shellfish gathering and fishing.

If you plan to dig for shellfish, find your way over to the town's Marine and Coastal Resources Department (508-228-7260) at 34 Washington Street or call this town office—often called the Marine Department. There, you can pick up a recreational shellfish license. At a cost of $25 for islanders and $100 for non-residents, the annual recreational shellfish license allows you to dig for steamers and quahogs, push-rake for scallops, collect oysters and mussels, and trap eels. Your recreational shellfish license spells out all the important information on seasons and limits, but you should always check with the Marine Department to make sure that these dates and amounts haven't changed. You should also ask the Marine Department about areas closed to shellfishing. Due to pollution from lawn fertilizers, bird waste, sewage, and boats, certain shellfishing areas are closed by the Marine Department when needed.

If fish is your goal, the following tackle shops will outfit you with the essential gear and point you toward some of the better onshore fishing spots: Bill Fisher Tackle, 14 New Lane, 508-228-2261; Barry Thurston's Tackle Shop, Candle and Salem Streets, 508-228-9595; Nantucket Tackle Center, 41 Sparks Avenue, 508-228-4081; Brant Point Marine, 32 Washington St, 508-228-6244; and Cross Rip Outfitters, 24 Easy St., 508-228-4900.

Wildlife

In your travels around Nantucket's wild lands, you'll likely encounter Nantucket wildlife. You may see deer bounding over the brush, white tails flipping with each leap, and you may even experience them up close, but, because they are nocturnal, they're likely observed only at dawn or dusk. There are no skunks or poisonous snakes on Nantucket, so you don't have those worries. However, should you explore areas near ponds and swamps, be wary of snapping turtles. These giants of Nantucket's turtle world are defined by their jagged shells with three distinct ridges running lengthwise, a long, jagged tail, and a huge head and hooked snout. These slow-moving turtles—females are typically seen far from their pond or stream habitats, searching for a spot to lay their eggs—will bite if provoked, so steer clear of this prehistoric amphibian.

If you choose to explore the cranberry bogs in spring through early summer, be aware that cranberry plants require honeybees to pollinate the cranberry flowers at that time of year. These bees can be very active. Look for signs posted to warn bog explorers of the dangers of the honeybees. People allergic to honey bee stings should avoid the bog walk until late summer through the cooler months, when the beehives are removed from the bog properties.

You will probably experience Nantucket's fauna most abundantly on and around the island's beaches. From late winter well into summer, shorebirds, specifically least terns and piping plovers nest and raise their young within several feet of the water. The tern is protected by the state as a Species of Special Concern, and the plover is protected by both the U.S. and the State as a Threatened Species. Harming the birds, their eggs, and their young is a major offense punishable by some serious jail time and fines that run into the thousands.

The Nantucket Conservation Foundation, Mass Audubon, the Trustees of Reservations, and the town's Marine and Coastal Resources Department work together to protect these shore birds from reckless beach drivers, unleashed dogs, kite fliers, and other predators. By the time these birds build their nests, signs warning people of their presence are posted, and in some cases, fences and wire exclosures are erected to protect them.

Give these birds a wide berth. Definitely bring your binoculars to watch them, and leash your dogs.

In spring and into summer, it's also common to see both harbor and gray seals up on the beaches either sunning themselves or resting. While adult shorebirds will just fly away as you approach their nests, think about why some people used to call seals "sea dogs." They may look as cute as a Labrador puppy, but they can apply a serious bite if you get too close.

If you spot a seal on the beach and it doesn't enter the water as you approach from a distance, there's a good chance something's wrong. It may be sick or injured—and as a result, short-tempered. Instead of approaching and possibly panicking a sick seal into flopping back into the water where it might drown, alert the Nantucket Mammal Stranding Team by calling the Nantucket Police Department at 508-228-1212. Tell them where and when you saw the seal and what its condition is, if you can, and they will call the Stranding Team immediately.

If you want to learn more about the natural world that you will see as you walk along, I recommend the following books (listed in the bibliography): *Field Guide to New England*, *Eastern Birds*, *Atlantic Seashore*, and *Nantucket Wildflowers*. Each will explain in greater detail the bird, animal, flower, or mollusk you saw while out walking.

Deer Ticks

You won't know when or where you picked up this miniature hitchhiker, but you may become aware of its bite after just a few days. The ticks that piggyback on deer, mice, dogs, and cats live in abundance wherever deer are found, such as on the edges of shrubby wooded areas, around marshes, in fields, and on dunes—all the places you'll be walking. No bigger than a period on this page, these little buggers carry, among other things, the dreaded Lyme disease.

A bacterial infection, Lyme disease can produce arthritic symptoms, and often the afflicted feel a sense of fatigue that no amount of sleep will cure. Other than spotting a deer tick on your body after a walk, the most telling sign that you've been bitten by an infected tick is a bull's-eye rash of red circles widening outward from the bite. Unfortunately for you, only about 40 percent of those infected ever get this rash. Since deer ticks in their larval and nymphal stages typically live on the ground and crawl upward once they find a host, check yourself from your shoes up, both during and after a walk.

Deer ticks are most potent with Lyme disease during those larval and nymphal stages, which occur in spring and summer, though the adults can also infect you. But you shouldn't let deer ticks keep you from walking about the island. Before you embark on each walk, apply bug repellent carefully, especially those products containing DEET. Put the repellent around your ankles and about half way up your calves—even if you're wearing socks and pants. To protect yourself further, tuck your pants into your socks.

When out on a walk through forested and brush-covered areas, stick to the trail. Stay away from tall grass, dense forest, and brush.

When you complete a walk, check your ankles and legs for ticks and then check your upper body as well, since the adults can be found on vegetation up to waist height. Remember that a deer tick usually wanders on your body 24 to 48 hours before it bites you and drops off, so you have time to spot and remove a tick before it bites. Be smart and check yourself often.

If you find no ticks but do find the rash—usually within two weeks after being bitten (use the date of the walk as a reference)—you can expect subdued flu-like symptoms to follow. These can include aches and pains, fever, sore throat, headache, chills, sore joints, and fatigue. If you know that you have been bitten by a tick or if you spot the rash or experience any of the symptoms, call your doctor immediately. On Nantucket, visit the emergency room at Nantucket Cottage Hospital, which handles outpatient removal of deer ticks. Most cases of early stage Lyme Disease are treated effectively with antibiotics, so don't delay.

What to Wear

The garb you'll need to enjoy the walks safely depends on when you're on island and how much time you have here. If you've done any walking at all, you know what works for you. But in case you don't, here, in order of importance, are my bare minimum suggestions for exploring Nantucket's wilderness:

— a comfortable pair of walking sneakers, shoes, or hiking boots
— shorts when it's hot, pants when it's cold or when you'll be walking in deer tick territory
— a windbreaker or light rain jacket
— a light-colored hat and sunglasses to ward off the sun
— any bug repellent product containing DEET (diethyltoluamide)
— sunblock with a sun protection factor (SPF) of at least 15

Getting Technical

A compass and working knowledge of its use will bolster your peace of mind when exploring any new lands, and it will also help you maintain your bearings if you stray from the walk maps. A light, compact pair of binoculars is good for spotting all the birds you're going to see on these walks.

Food and Water

The other thing you should be sure to take with you is a water bottle. Your water dispenser alternatives range from the ubiquitous plastic squeeze bottles to the convenient nylon bladders that are carried inside a slim backpack from which a plastic tube runs out and down over your shoulder, enabling you to sip from the hose as you walk along.

After your water supply, your body's fuel should be your next crucial choice. I usually bring along fruit and/or a sports energy bar.

It may not seem like it, but walking is good exercise that will dip deeply into your energy supply. Drink at least a large glass of water or fruit juice before you embark, then drink at regular intervals during the walk. I just take little sips from my water supply as I walk along, and when I reach the halfway point in the walk, I eat whatever I brought with me to fuel the walk back. Your walking diet depends on your own needs.

Pack out what you pack in

In case you're unfamiliar with this overused but never out of style phrase, please don't leave your trash behind; bring it back out with you. Don't even leave your banana peels, orange rinds, or cigarette butts. The reason you're here is to see this relatively pristine island and its natural environment. How tough is it to carry your waste back to a trash barrel? And don't just stop with carrying out your own waste: if you see some less conscientious individual's trash along the way and have room for it in your pack, by all means help keep Nantucket clean.

Walk at Your Own Risk

When you venture out on any of the walking routes in *Walking Nantucket*, remember *that you walk at your own risk*, and should expect to deal with any and all problems that might arise along the routes in this book. Your children should never be unsupervised. As a responsible walker, exercise caution, good sense, and respect of people you encounter on these walks, property, wildlife, and vegetation at all times. Even the most enjoyable of days can be ruined by sunburn, animal or insect bites, or accidents; disregard of safety and environmental regulations, and altercations with private property owners will get you into even more trouble.

If you accidentally stray onto private land, be respectful and walk back off the same way you came. Do not walk up beach stairs and private paths, and do not go through private yards or driveways to access the beach. No Trespassing signs mean what they say—obey them! Some private land owners, especially various conservation groups may allow the public to walk their lands. This permission can be revoked at any time, so before starting out on your walk, check to see what rules and regulations these land owners have established, and follow them. Remember, when you head out onto Nantucket's beautiful shore and inland areas, give them the care and respect you would give your own land.

Don't Miss These Walks!

If you weren't born on the island or are unable to live here year-round, it will be tough to walk all of the routes in *Walking Nantucket* on just one visit, even if you're one of the lucky ones who stay through the whole summer season. To help narrow down your selection, I've selected a short list of walks that I think you ought not to leave the island without experiencing.

If you have only a day or a weekend to explore Nantucket, don't return home without walking around Sanford Farm. With just a little more time, try to work in the 'Sconset Bluff Walk, The Creeks at low tide, or Masquetuck. Walkers with a week or more on the island should definitely try to work in all four of the above walks and also walk Coskata, the Windswept Cranberry Bogs walks, Tupancy Links, and Lily Pond-Grove Lane.

However, these are simply suggestions on how to sample Nantucket in a short period of time based on the parts of Nantucket I think will give walkers the most varied look at our island. You may have your own agenda and therefore should feel completely free to do whichever walks tickle your feet the most.

Enjoy the walks!

Shorelines

The three great elemental sounds in nature are the sound of the rain, the sound of the wind, and the sound of the outer ocean on a beach. I have heard them all and that of the ocean is the most awesome, beautiful and varied...
— Henry Beston, The Outer Most House

Shorelines + Walks

29 + Capaum Pond

35 + Coskata Pond

43 + Eel Point-North Point

51 + Little Neck

57 + The Creeks

63 + Polpis Harbor Boat Landing

69 + Quidnet-Sesachacha

75 + Smith's Point

LONG-TAILED DUCK

Difficulty Rating: *
Dogs: Yes
Children: Yes

The Area

The site of the island's first organized town, Sherburne, is on Nantucket's north shore. What remains of the original island harbor is now Capaum Pond, a semi-salt pond surrounded by cattails and private land with modern houses on three sides and Nantucket Sound to the north.

Founded in 1659 by the island's first settlers and named after the town in England from which settler John Gardner's family emigrated, the buildings and homes of Sherburne sat perched around their tiny harbor for about 30 years. Around 1712, after decades of shifting shoals slowly clogging the harbor entrance, a violent storm pushed tons of sand into the channel and sealed Sherburne Harbor for good.

Over the next few decades, Sherburne residents gradually moved their homes onto the shores around today's harbor. You can see one of these houses, originally owned by the Starbuck Family, at the corner of Gardner and Main streets opposite the Civil War Monument, where it currently serves as a private residence.

If you crave more information about Sherburne Village, you'll find it at the Peter Foulger Museum at 15 Broad St. in downtown Nantucket.

What You'll See

The remains of Sherburne and its harbor, land now owned by the Nantucket Conservation Foundation, are at the end of Washing Pond Road. A dirt road becomes a sand trail and leads to the water, but be sure not to miss the pond on your way to the beach for a swim. From the dune to the left of the sand trail leading to the beach, you'll get a good look at this pond that is completely separated from Nantucket Sound by a barrier beach of dunes, beach grass, bayberry, poison ivy, and cattails. You'll also get a sense of the size of the old Sherburne community.

The Nantucket Conservation Foundation owns the beach immediately in front of the pond. This beach is perfect for families with small children, because the water is warm and shallow and the Sound doesn't produce the waves and pounding surf of the island's south shore. It's also an easy walk for those who would rather avoid a long, strenuous hike over dunes to the beach.

When to Go

Summer is the obvious season to explore this part of the island, but in winter, fall, and early spring, when most the shrubs and trees are bare, you can see more of the pond. However, the prevailing winter winds are north, northwest, northeast, and east, so be prepared on chilly, blustery days with warm clothing and boots.

I also love to go on a warm foggy morning or at dusk when you can hear the foghorns at the entrance to Nantucket Harbor. When there's no sound but the horn, the wind, and the gulls calling in the mist, and you can't see any trace of the 21st century, you can transport yourself back in time. Sit facing Capaum Pond and try to imagine what it was like for Tristram Coffin, Thomas Macy, Edward Starbuck, Peter Foulger, John Gardner, John Swain, Jr., John Coleman, Richard Gardner, Christopher

Hussey, and William Bunker to form and found a town, and then to have to work out the logistics of moving it three miles east.

The Walk

More of a trip to the beach, than a walk along a trail into the wilds of Nantucket, Capaum Pond is part of this book because of the significance of its island history. From the beach parking area, walk toward the pond to get a good look at it while imagining how the houses were laid out around it. Walk down to the beach by finding the trail through the dunes at the north end of the parking area. Walking along the beach is also an option, but remember that this beach is bounded east and west by private property.

You may also want to walk back out the way you came in and out along Washing Pond Road for decent views of the island west of the water tower.

Getting There

Capaum Pond is easily found at the end of Washing Pond Road, which is 1.5 miles from town on Cliff Road. Travel out of town on Cliff Road, which starts at the intersection of Easton, North Water, and Chester streets. Cyclists starting in town should use caution, because Cliff Road's bike path doesn't start until just after Crooked Lane about a half mile out of town. Once you pass Crooked Lane, walk approximately another half mile, following the split rail fence along the bike path past the open land on the north side of the road, past the gravel parking area of Tupancy Links, and up around a right bend to Washing Pond Road. Those using NRTA's Madaket route should get off at the Eel Point Road stop and walk east along the Cliff Road bike path to reach Washing Pond Road, about a half mile toward town. When you reach the water tower, you've found Washing Pond Road.

Turn north on Washing Pond Road and follow the road as it bends to the west—the water tower will be on your left. When the pavement ends, pass the wooden sign for Old Harbor Road on the left and walk along the dirt road to the right, straight into a pine grove. This short dirt road curves to the right and ends in a parking area with a sand trail leading to the beach. If this lot is full, go back out to Cliff Road, turn left, and go about 200 yards to the Tupancy Links parking lot for additional parking. Walk back to Washing Pond Road and follow the above instructions to get to Capaum Pond and its beach.

Coskata Pond
2.9 miles

Difficulty Rating: ***
Dogs: Yes (leashed)
Children: Yes

The Area

My urban friend, who rarely gets to see the shore birds I commune with all summer long, joined me for a walk out to Coskata Pond and Haulover Pond one summer. When he spotted a pair of orange-beaked oystercatchers flying low over the falling tide, making their peep-peep-peep call in time with every wing beat, he was in awe.

This barrier beach system is jointly owned and managed by the Nantucket Conservation Foundation and the Trustees of Reservations, both of which operate out of the guard shack off Wauwinet Road just before the Wauwinet Inn. From their shack in a dirt parking lot, they sell Oversand Vehicle Permits to four-wheel drivers and dispense vital "do's and don'ts" to those venturing out to Coatue, Coskata, and Great Point.

What You'll See

Bird life abounds in and around Haulover Pond, Coskata Pond, and its surrounding woods during all seasons. In the spring through early fall, I've regularly spotted whimbrels, plovers, sandpipers, oystercatchers, great blue herons, black-capped night herons, little egrets, snowy egrets, great egrets, nesting ospreys, cormorants and, of course, herring and black-backed gulls. And in the winter, the Head of the Harbor, Haulover Pond, and Coskata Pond form a refuge for sea ducks such as white-winged scoters, long-tailed ducks, eiders, loons, and mergansers along with mallards and black ducks.

The wildlife you'll see at the Haulover Pond enjoys sanctuary at this tidal wonder, thanks to a powerful nor'easter in December 1896 that tore a hole in the dune—from the ocean to the harbor—near the last few houses nestled precariously in the dunes just beyond the Wauwinet Inn. The churning Atlantic Ocean had an easy time of it, because for years, Nantucket fishermen hauled their fishing dories over the narrowest part of this barrier beach, slowly cutting a shallow trench between ocean and harbor—hence the name, "Haulover."

For 12 years, as a result of the storm, the ocean-to-harbor cut persisted, allowing fishermen to row their dories through the hole and back into the harbor, saving them the time and energy it took to pull their dories over the dunes.

Haulover Pond eventually evolved as sand gradually closed the gap between ocean and harbor. The beach on the north eroded while the beach behind it built up until the water encountered the clay and gravel of the Coskata Woods, which halted further erosion and allowed sand to fill in the hole. What remains today is a pond, surrounded by a saltmarsh that will drain almost completely when the moon is full.

As you walk to the left (northwest) of Haulover Pond, Coskata Pond and the Woods will gradually come into view. Before you reach Coskata—likely an Algonquian word combining *kowaw* for "pine," *htugk* for "'tree," and *ut* for "'at": "at the pine trees"—you'll see signs posted in spring and summer warning you that endangered shore birds, including piping plovers and least terns, are nesting in this area. Call the Nantucket Conservation Foundation or consult the staff at the gatehouse to learn which birds, if any, are active. Usually the signs prohibit just beach drivers from proceeding, but sometimes walkers are told to keep out as well. Heed these warnings when you see them and return later in the summer when the birds' chicks have fledged. Also, if you bring your dog, keep it leashed

as you pass near the Haulover Pond, because this is where the plovers and terns typically nest.

Before you reach Coskata Pond just beyond its low bluffs, you may want to venture into the woods. But know this: the ghost of a long dead island Native American named Mudturtle can sometimes be seen in the early morning or evening fog during the winter, wafting through the woods. It's rumored that Mudturtle kidnapped an island Indian princess from her Coatue home and swept her away to his cave carved into the bluff overlooking the harbor. Mudturtle, of the Taumkaud tribe, worshiped from afar the daughter of the King of the Khauds on Coatue, and when he heard she was to marry a young sachem, he hatched a plan to kidnap the woman he desired.

Capturing her at night, Mudturtle swept her off to his cave carved into the Coskata bluff overlooking the harbor, but by morning, his prize had escaped and run back to her village. When her father heard of Mudturtle's transgression, he formed a posse to hunt down the crazed Taumkaud. But the incredulous band could not find Mudturtle. Soon, the Coskata recluse washed up dead on the beach below his cave. A fatal wound, likely inflicted by an arrow when Mudturtle fled the Khaud village, was deemed the cause of death. When Mudturtle's pursuers tried to bury him face down in the sand at low tide, his body washed up on the beach three times before the Khauds could sink him deep enough into the harbor floor.

Although I have not seen the specter of Mudturtle, once, while I walked through the woods on a winter sunset jaunt, a large snowy owl burst out of the brush about 10 feet from me, jolting my heart into my mouth and flashing an image of Mudturtle's wispy shadow across my mind's eye.

When to Go

In summer, I always enjoy this walk at low tide and without shoes, because it's fun to wade up the channel into Coskata Pond and then float down into the harbor on the outgoing tide. In fall and winter, this inter-tidal zone is a way station for migrating birds. Take your pick of seasons. If you choose summer, don't forget bug repellent. Mosquitoes and no-see-ums are present at all times when the wind dies and, the dreaded greenhead flies of late June into July employ a stabbing bite.

In spring, horseshoe crabs are thinking "family." As you pick your way along the shore, keep your eyes open for the smaller males catching piggyback rides on the larger females as they mate in the shallows. Unfortunately, their shoreline procreation can be their undoing, because gulls will drag them out of the water, flip them over and eat them as if from a bowl. Their gutted shells, along with those of spider, green, and other crabs, litter the beach throughout spring and summer.

You can walk this beach anytime in the year, but if you choose late fall through early spring and intend to cross the shallow yet chilly mouth of Haulover Pond, or the mouth of Coskata to reach Coatue, wear waterproof boots. An autumn walk will reward you with color: because Nantucket lacks the extensive hardwood forests of the mainland, the woods at Coskata, comprised of oaks, maples, black tupelos, and cedars, is one of only a few island groves that develops true fall foliage.

The Walk

Park your transportation in the designated area next to the Trustees of Reservations and Nantucket Conservation Foundation shack and walk north on Wauwinet Road. Passing the Wauwinet Inn on the left, follow the sand and dirt road out past the beach houses on the east side of the road. About 200 yards beyond the last house, where the packed sand turns to soft, deep sand, turn left (west) at the first intersection that you come to. A right turn (east) will lead you out to the ocean beach.

This sand trail toward the harbor snakes through the low dunes of bayberry, poison ivy, beach grass, *Rosa rugosa*, and saltmarsh cordgrass, and past the Haulover Pond. A word to the walking wise: do not try to walk over the vegetation between the sand trail and the pond. The mud of the saltmarsh surrounding the pond is not unlike quicksand, and its vegetation is quite vulnerable to foot traffic.

The sand trail will end in a split just as you reach the beach. Choose the left (southeast) path if your intention is to investigate Haulover Pond or straight if you want to walk directly to the opening of Coskata Pond. If your plan is to walk through the woods, take the right path, inland from the harbor, toward an old telephone pole at the edge of the forest, marking the opening of a trail surrounded by cedar trees. The trail through the woods will lead you out to the southeast side of the pond. You can either wade out to the beach in waist deep water or backtrack to the cedars and the telephone pole and then explore the mouth of the pond. Once you reach the spot where you entered the woods, head right (northwest) along the low bluff overlooking the harbor and pick your way along the rocks out to mouth of Coskata Pond.

To return to the Wauwinet gatehouse parking lot, retrace the sand road the way you came and follow the beach road past Haulover Pond, now on your right, to the main beach trail and back to civilization.

Getting There

The Trustees of Reservations and Nantucket Conservation Foundation's gatehouse and parking lot are at the end of Wauwinet Road. Take Polpis Road or its bike path from Milestone Road for about 3.5 miles, until you see the left turn for Wauwinet Road, marked by a turquoise town sign.

For NRTA riders, the nearest stop is the Wauwinet Road stop on the 'Sconset Route via Polpis Road; from there, it is a considerable hike of roughly 2.5 miles to the gatehouse.

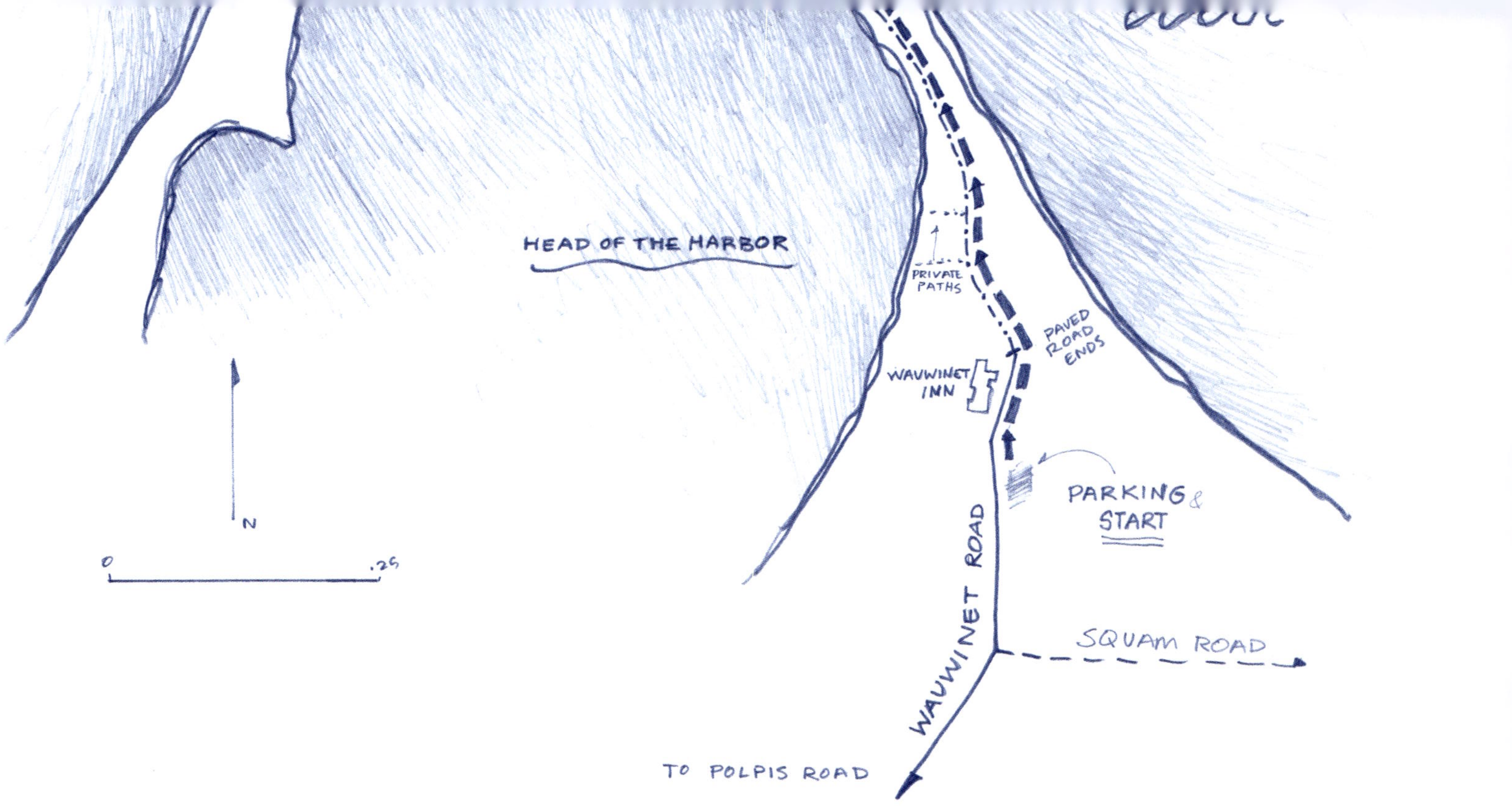

40 • WALKING NANTUCKET • COSKATA POND

HEAD OF THE HARBOR

WAUWINET INN

PRIVATE PATHS

PAVED ROAD ENDS

WAUWINET ROAD

TO POLPIS ROAD

PARKING & START

SQUAM ROAD

N

0

.25

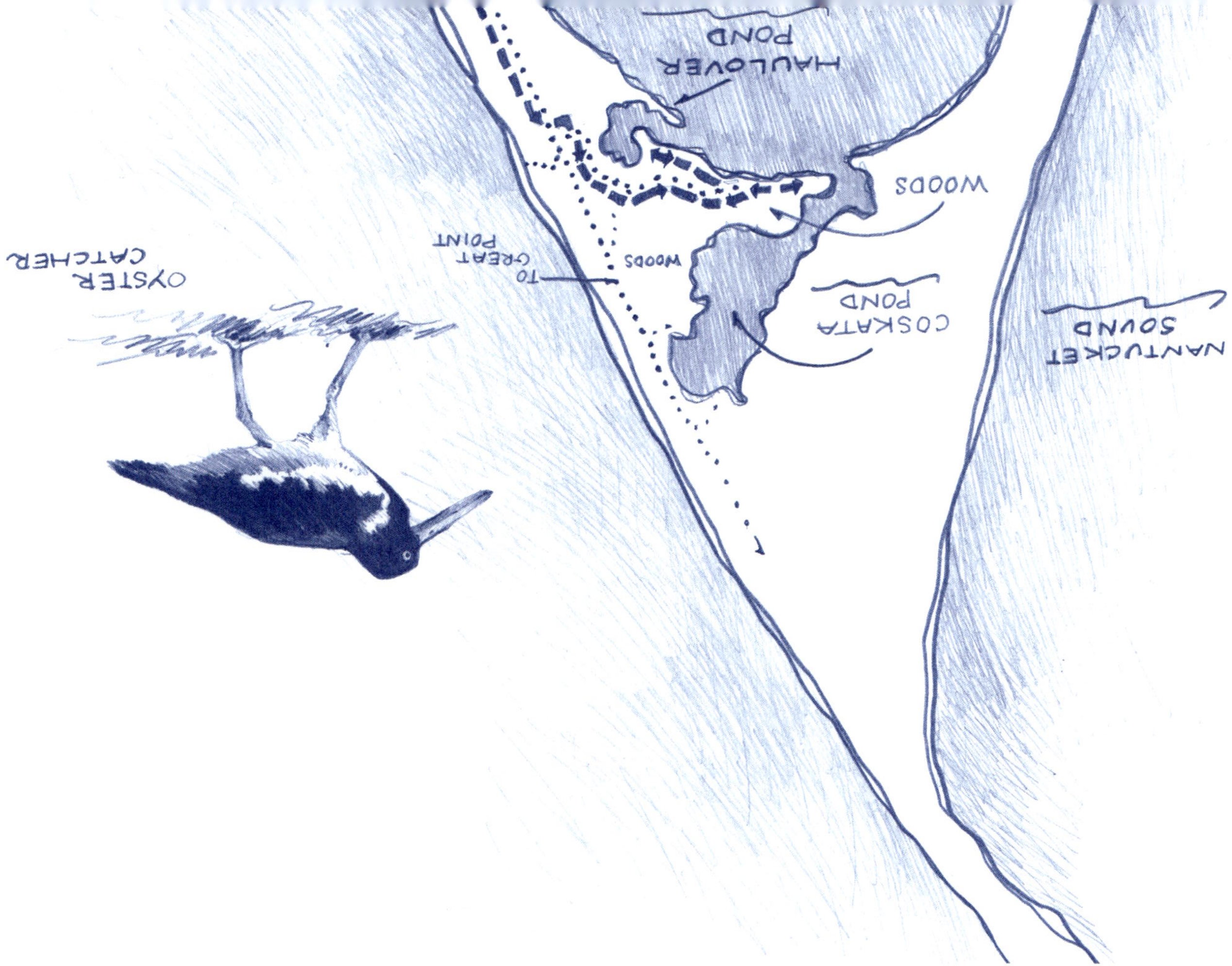

11 • WALKING NANTUCKET • COSKATA POND

NANTUCKET SOUND

WOODS

COSKATA POND

HAULOVER POND

WOODS

TO GREAT POINT

OYSTER CATCHER

Eel Point – North Point

2.4 miles *2.3 miles*

Sand Road to Eel Point
Difficulty Rating: ***
Dogs: Yes
Children: Yes

North Point-Eel Point Loop
Difficulty Rating: ***
Dogs: Yes
Children: Yes

The Area

After just a few trips out to these two dune fields studded with beaches and surrounded in summer by deliciously warm water, you'll be pleasantly bewildered by the low number of people who frequent Nantucket's northwestern peninsula. Sure, those with striped bass trophies over their desks and "Think Bluefish" bumper stickers on their cars will always suit up in their waders and inch their way out onto the flats—known as "the Bathtubs" for the warm shallow tidal pools that both fish and children love—between Eel Point and North Point. But most people tend to gravitate toward the South Shore beaches in summer, and this part of the island is left largely to the fish seekers, whether feathered or neoprene-clad, and a few quahoggers who know where the best littlenecks and chowders hide.

For walkers in the warmer months, you need only bare feet and a dead low tide to reap the splendor of this beautiful spot. Of course, a perfect sunset and a light breeze don't hurt either.

What You'll See

During the summer, you should spend about three or four hours out here to soak up this beach stroll completely, but if your motive is to enjoy a good scenic pre-breakfast or after-dinner walk during which you can take in Madaket Harbor, Esther's Island, Smith's Point, Tuckernuck Island, and, on clear cobalt blue days, Muskeget Island, then you can easily see it all in about 90 minutes.

These two jaunts can be a self-taught lesson in Nantucket harbor plant and animal life. If you want to identify everything you'll see, *Walking Nantucket* bibliography (page 223) lists a number of reference books, available at island bookstores, that describe in more detail the various shore plants, animals, and birds.

These Eel and North Point walks lead to beaches not frequented by the surf-loving crowd that flocks to the South Shore and is relatively uncrowded in the warmer months. However, be aware that, while following these routes, you will be sharing space with the voracious mosquito. Looking south from the sand road, you'll notice the marsh is cross-hatched with narrow ditches that run from nearby out to the harbor. These ditches were dug by the town many years ago to control the mosquitoes that lay their eggs at the edges of ponds and in saltmarshes. When the ditches fill in with the rising tide, small fish swim in and eat the eggs of the mosquitoes. Unfortunately, it's an unreliable form of population control. Because the minnows can't get all of the eggs, and unless there's a moderate breeze blowing, you should lather yourself in bug repellent. Anything containing DEET will do, including any of the several sunblock products that now contain DEET along with their sunscreen ingredients.

This sand trail out to Eel Point is perfect for watching the northern harrier hunt for rodents, baby birds, and frogs. A raptor, the northern harrier—formerly known as the marsh hawk—has a longer body and wings spaced closer to its head than most hawks. Bands of white feathers at the base of its wings and its tail make this bird easy to spot as it hovers low—sometimes only several feet—over the ground. Look for it cruising the saltmarsh between you and the harbor and sometimes in the dunes.

Out on the shoreline, you're likely to see whimbrels, lesser yellow legs, little egrets, black-crowned night herons, American oystercatchers with bright orange bills, terns of several varieties, cormorants, great blue herons, and gulls.

From late spring through early fall, if you choose to walk at low tide, you've picked the right time to enjoy the Bathtubs. The tip of North Point becomes partially exposed at low tide as the warm water rushes out into the Sound, revealing the Bathtubs—shallow pools of water with sandy bottoms that are perfect for wading and sitting in to cool off. Do remember, however, that you don't control the water level of the Bathtubs as you do in your own tub at home. Keep an eye on the tide and don't swim in water over your head. The six- to eight-knot current coursing between this beach and Tuckernuck will whisk you out to sea or out into Nantucket Sound before you realize where you are.

When to Go

Wind and cold and rain are the triple threat of the exposed, unprotected parts of Nantucket during fall and winter. Therefore, walks on North Point and Eel Point are best during spring, summer, and early fall. Besides, since you'll be walking along the water, isn't wonderful to know that you can jump or wade into the ocean whenever the mood hits you?

Go when it's hot out so you can swim in the Bathtubs. Go at sunset in the summer with a surfcasting rod and catch bluefish. Go when spring has sprung to experience the saltmarsh coming alive. Go in autumn on a hazy warm day and enjoy the delightful air unpolluted with biting insects. Just go when the mood hits you.

The Walks:
Sand Road to Eel Point

From atop the bank near the parking spots, you'll be able to see out over the saltmarsh along the northern shore of Madaket Harbor, all of the dunes leading out to Eel and North Point, and the islands of Tuckernuck and Muskeget beyond. Begin your explorations by leaving the parking area via the sand road that drops down into the saltmarsh and heads briefly northwest toward the dunes.

About 100 yards along, you'll reach a split in the road. Go left, roughly west, and walk on the sand road, keeping the harbor and the saltmarsh on your left and the dunes on your right.

By following this sand trail, you can't help but run into Eel Point. Stay on the road as it meanders toward and finally dead-ends into the beach. The road passes several cuts in the dunes leading to the beach, so follow your nose through whichever cut in the dunes appeals to you to reach the beach.

From the end of this beach road facing south to Smith's Point on the other side Madaket Harbor, you can enjoy a stroll east along the beach, back toward the inner harbor, exploring the sand spit that sweeps into the harbor. Once on the spit, take your time beachcombing as you approach a deep, narrow channel that separates the tip of the sand spit from the saltmarsh.

Getting back to your transportation is easy: follow the path back the way you came.

North Point-Eel Point Loop

Should you wish to spend more time on the sand in a loop walk, take the other choice at the split in the sand road just after the parking area: go straight and follow this road through the dunes and out onto a beach that faces Nantucket Sound. Then walk left heading west along the beach, toward Tuckernuck Island.

During summer, the Nantucket Conservation Foundation, which owns most of the undeveloped portion of Eel and North points, usually closes off either or both points to vehicles—and sometimes walkers—to protect nesting least terns and piping plovers. When you encounter signs to this effect, respect and heed their warnings.

If no such warnings are posted, walk on as the beach arcs southward past North Point and within sight of Smith's Point across Madaket Harbor. The shallow water facing Tuckernuck Island is what is known as the Bathtubs.

Once you've explored the Bathtubs, take your time walking away from North Point heading south down the beach to Eel Point. At dead low tide, you'll walk across sand and mud flats covered with shallow tepid sea water and in the summer, if you love more than just laying on the beach, you'll revel in the wonders of exploring this intertidal zone.

Walk just beyond the flats and you'll find Eel Point and the sand road that will complete your loop back to the parking area. If you want to explore more of Eel Point, use the directions for the Eel Point walk for guidance. Otherwise, find any trail leading away from the beach after the flats and follow it back to the main sand trail that is in sight of the saltmarsh on your right (south) and the dunes on your left (north). This road will end at a "T" intersection. Turn right and follow the path up to the parking lot and, just beyond, Eel Point and Warren's Landing roads.

Getting There

To reach the starting point of this walk, you have a choice of two roads of different degrees of washboard-pothole bumpiness. If you don't mind the pounding your vehicle takes on Nantucket's questionable dirt tracks, use Eel Point Road, off Madaket Road just west of the Cliff Road intersection. If you want to spare your joints or your vehicle, or you're just in a hurry, continue on Madaket Road to Warren's Landing Road, after the Nantucket Landfill and First Bridge.

If you've selected Eel Point Road, follow it to its sandy end. At the sharpest turn the road takes (to the left and to the south), head up and to the right, roughly northwest between several houses. Once up on this rise, you'll find a small parking area for two larger or three smaller cars.

Warren's Landing Road is found on the northwest side of Madaket Road between First Bridge and Second Bridge. Wind your way through a pine grove dotted with houses as the road turns sharply right then left, and then becomes a dirt road. Continue on as it slowly rises, offering views of Madaket Harbor to the south and west. Warren's Landing Road will then drop slowly, meeting the western end of Eel Point Road. Before a sharp right turn to the east, travel left up a small rise to the parking area. NRTA bus riders should take the Madaket bus, get off at the Warren's Landing Road stop, and walk in following these same directions.

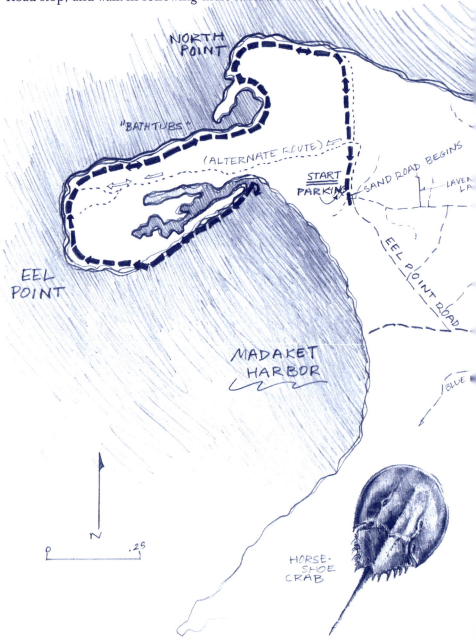

.8 miles

Difficulty Rating: *
Dogs: Yes
Children: Yes

The Area

Jutting out between Hither Creek to the east and Madaket Harbor to the west is a peninsula well worth including in your explorations of the island's western village. Little Neck, the sixth property that the Nantucket Conservation Foundation purchased after its inception in 1963, is a coastal beach/sand dune habitat where you can watch the long-tailed ducks (formerly called oldsquaw) fly in from their winter feeding grounds off Nantucket's South Shore.

What You'll See

The long-tailed duck, which spends a majority of its life on the water, goes ashore only on tundra ponds in Alaska and the Canadian Arctic to breed, but it flies over Nantucket's southwestern end every afternoon during the winter. The name oldsquaw was recently changed to long-tailed duck because of its negative connotation toward Native Americans.

Some of my birding friends travel to Madaket several times a week in the fall and winter to watch the ducks on their daily commute. During the day, they dive for fish in the ocean ten-to-twenty miles off Nantucket. Late in the afternoon, they flap their way back to Nantucket Sound to form large flotillas in which they sleep during the night.

You can spot this airborne stream of ducks—a miles-long black swath of squawking feathery specks with long string-like tail feathers—from anywhere on Madaket's shores, and from almost anywhere along Nantucket's South

Shore. But Little Neck is a particularly advantageous observation spot, because these ducks tend to fly right over Hither Creek and Madaket Harbor—low enough for you to hear their in-flight conversations.

Birds other than the long-tailed duck abound on this walk, many more in the fall and winter months when Nantucket becomes a migratory rest stop and winter home for multitudes of land and water birds. Great blue herons regularly wade along the shores, among ducks like eiders, buffle-heads, golden eyes, mallards, skoaters, and mergansers in the waters around Little Neck.

This 23.1-acre tract of bayberry, beach grass, and goldenrod is an excellent place to see the extraordinary Madaket sunsets because of the way the sun's fading rays play on the various bodies of water around Little Neck. And although Warren's Landing is a great place to go for the western Nantucket sunset experience, you have to get out of your car to fully appreciate the symphony of colors at day's end.

Little Neck is also an ideal spot for stargazing on a clear night, since it is a good six to seven miles from the glow of town.

When To Go

Little Neck is an exposed nub of a peninsula that is perfect for sunset walks spring, summer and early fall. But when the temperatures drop and the northeast, east, and north winds that put the chill on Nantucket for four or five months blow in, choose another walk. Beach roses will be blooming in spring and throughout the summer. If you do like winter walks, the many varieties of ducks and other shore birds mentioned above love the sheltered waters of Hitcher Creek and the mouth of Madaket Harbor.

The Walk

At dead low tide, you can make a circuit out of this walk by picking your way along a narrow beach strewn with mounds of dead eelgrass and bordered by rushes and beach grass. Even a half-tide, though, makes the beach part of this walk passable only if you are willing to get your feet wet. So, if a loop is a must and you're walking between early June and mid-October, you'll have no trouble wading through the warm harbor water. If you slosh along barefoot without some sort of rubber sandals, be careful of shell pieces that can easily cut your feet.

However, if the tide is high or nearly so, your best choice is to walk back out to Little Neck Way, take the left fork and follow the road to its terminus. This makes for a short in-and-out walk, but one well worth taking, since you can really see a lot of Madaket in about 20 minutes.

From the fork marked by one of the Nantucket Conservation Foundation's maroon property posts, Little Neck Way quickly turns to a sand trail with thickets of bayberry and *Rosa rugosa* growing on either side. After just a few minutes of walking, Hither Creek will appear to the east over the dunes, and the village of Madaket can be seen just on the edges of its shores. And about halfway along this road, you'll also be able to see Smith's Point to the southwest, Tuckernuck Island to the west, Eel Point to the northwest, and all of Madaket Harbor.

Get back to your transportation, and North Cambridge Street by walking north away from the harbor end of Little Neck. Or, walk (or wade) back along the outside shore with Jackson Point on your left, and Madaket Harbor beyond, on your left until you reach the grass parking area.

Getting There

From Caton Circle at the western end of Upper Main Street, travel west on Madaket Road or its bike path. Turn right on North Cambridge Street. If you lack a bike or a car, catch NRTA's Madaket bus from town to the Cambridge Street stop. From this stop, walk west on North Cambridge Street.

About two tenths of a mile from Madaket Road is a left turn, the first left after the boatyard road. Take this left and follow the narrow, rolling track to the third right, marked by one of the Nantucket Conservation

Foundation's maroon posts, which will lead you to a small, grassy parking area overlooking Madaket Harbor. However, the parking area is small, and if full, you should try another walk or park along Ames Avenue at the end of Madaket Road, walking back along the bike path to North Cambridge Street to begin this walk. Also, be sensitive to the neighbors of this open space and do not drive up driveways or make a lot of noise.

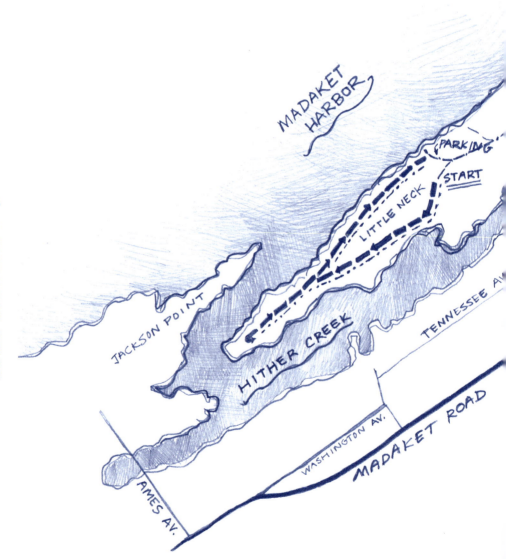

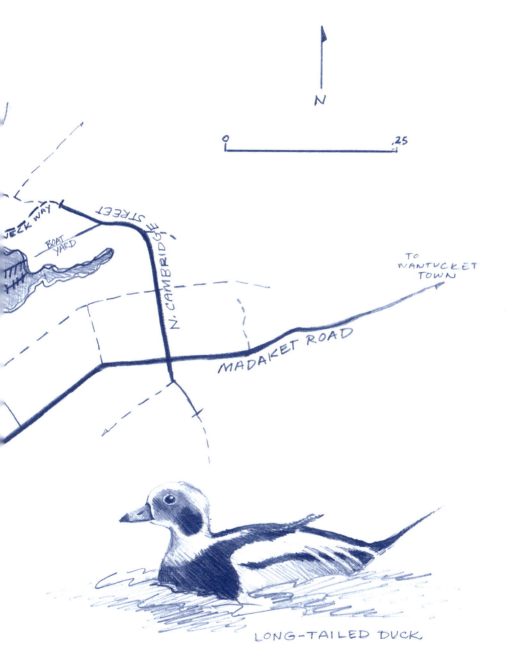

The Creeks

.5 miles

Difficulty Rating: *
Dogs: Yes (leashed)
Children: Yes

The Area

Looking out into the harbor from Washington Street, it's easy to think that you'll never get the kind of access to Nantucket Harbor that boat owners enjoy. With only a few public access points—at Brant Point, the boat basin, the town pier, Children's Beach and Washington Street Extension—many people experience that so-close-and-yet-so-far feeling of being held at arm's length from the natural beauty of the harbor. From this harborside street, you can catch fleeting glimpses out into the mass of boats and the upper harbor beyond, but you can't really see enough.

That is, not until you discover the trail out to the Creeks and the mudflats between the beach and saltmarsh at the end of Washington Street Extension. Even I didn't think of walking there at first. The small beach is one of my favorite places to launch my kayak for harbor expeditions and many people keep their dinghies there for access to boats moored just off shore.

Surrounded on three sides by houses, Our Island Home (Nantucket's nursing home), and Marine Home Center, the Creeks are a precious natural jewel of saltmarsh cordgrass with a ribbon of warm harbor water snaking through—a sanctuary for birds and other estuarine creatures seeking a relatively quiet area in an otherwise bustling harbor.

As an ecosystem, the Creeks area is essentially a saltmarsh. Saltmarshes are intertidal areas where, twice daily, flood tides submerge the low marsh and, twice daily, ebb tides expose it again.

Grasses and salt-tolerant vegetation called halophytes dominate this marsh. These plants have a specialized mechanism that rapidly increases the salinity of the plant's tissue in response to increased salinity surrounding its roots. They also tend to develop fleshy stems and leaves and salt-secreting glands that help the halophyte keep the salt solution from becoming too strong.

From an ecological standpoint, these wetlands serve as a microbial filter, with bacteria and plants naturally cleansing the toxins from the harbor water by breaking them down into usable nutrients, and acting as a sponge for storm surge when hurricanes and nor'easters strike the island. As you approach the Creeks, the first thing you'll notice—other than the splendid, sweeping views of town, the old mill, the harbor, the boats, Brant Point, Coatue, and Monomoy—is the smell. That pungent mud flat aroma is as sweet as the smell of springtime beach rose blossoms to my nose, and if you don't already love poking around the shore at low tide, it will soon be as fragrant to you. It is the smell of decomposing marine plants and animals, from tiny plankton to beach grass, from quahogs and crabs to birds and small mammals. Its bouquet means there is a healthy lifecycle present.

What You'll See

Great egrets, snowy egrets, great blue herons, black-crowned night herons, whimbrels, ducks of many varieties, Canada Geese, and scores of other winged species live and feed in the Creeks. However, since the saltmarsh is also an ideal breeding spot for mosquitoes, greenheads, and other flying nasties, from spring through the end of summer, bug repellent is strongly recommended.

How deep you dive into this experience is up to you. However, when you do this walk at high tide, do not attempt to cross the mouth of the channel leading into the Creeks. Although not too deep at high tide, the current is swift. Also, don't try to venture out on the grass in the Creeks. As resilient as they are to violent ocean storms and pollution, the plants and creatures living in the honeycomb network of mud, soil, and roots that make up this soggy terra firma can be irreparably damaged by foot traffic.

When to Go

Summer is the ideal time for this walk, because the warm water is perfect for wading at either low or high tide. And because when the tide goes out, the mudflats between the beach and Monomoy are exposed, granting walkers splendid views of the harbor only afforded to those with boats. But if you go year-round, you can see how the harbor and the Creeks change through the seasons, even observing from the beach and trail. Because of the fragile structure of mud, grass, and roots that make up the Creeks, explore this saltwater marsh only by canoe, rowboat, or kayak.

If on foot, bring binoculars to observe the natural beauty of the Creeks from afar. The beach is narrow and the path to the Creeks is short, ending at a small point at the opening to the Creeks' waterway. A high tide walk means either wading close to shore in the warmer months or walking down the path to view the Creeks and spot birds.

Low-tide walkers from early summer through early fall can explore both the beach area and exposed mud flats.

The Walk

At the end of Washington Street Extension, walk along the south side of the town's man-made wetland protected by a split-rail fence. Just before you reach the tiny beach with dinghies scattered about, go right (southeast) down a sand path along the shore. There's small house with a deck facing toward the harbor to the right. Walk toward the Creeks, following the trail to its end where it overlooks the saltmarsh.

If you're walking at low tide during late spring, summer, and early fall, you can wade and walk out on the mud flats at your leisure.

Getting There

From town, follow Washington Street along the harbor past the town pier. Keep going straight past the turn for Francis Street, passing Francis Street Beach as Washington Street becomes Washington Street Extension. Once past the boat yard on the left and Sayle's Seafood on the right, parking in front of the split-rail fence surrounding the wetland, and along its south side. From the Rotary, follow Orange Street north into town. Go right onto Union Street, and at the sign for Steamboat Wharf, go right onto Francis Street. At the t-intersection facing the harbor, go right onto Washington Street Extension and follow the above directions.

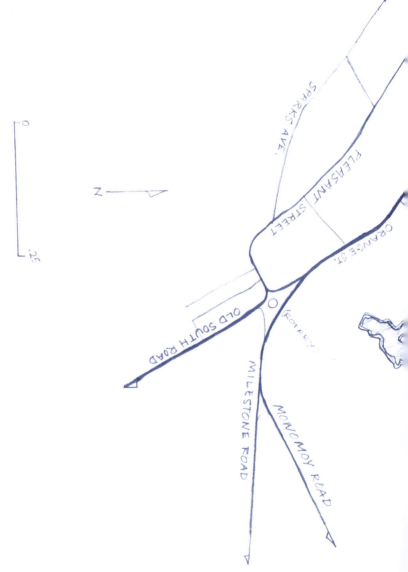

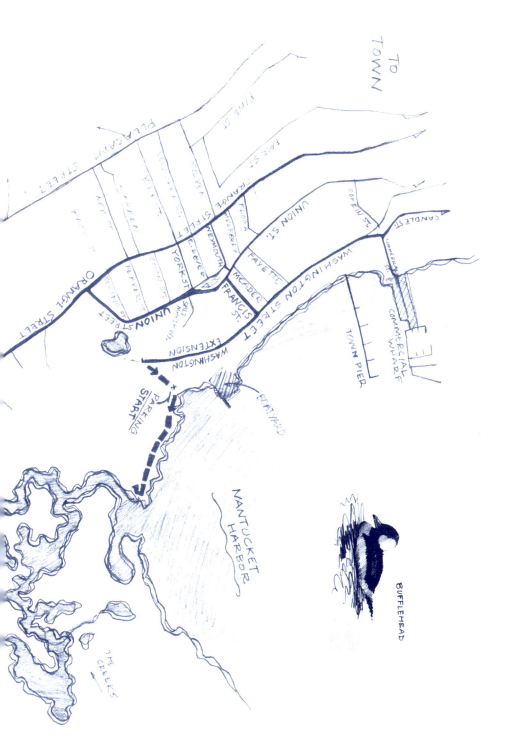

Polpis Harbor Boat Landing
.9 miles

Difficulty Rating: **
Dogs: Yes
Children: Yes

The Area

If you really want to experience the lifecycle of intertidal marine life through your nose, get out to Polpis Harbor. Just the slightest breeze can fill your nostrils with the delicious, heady smell of the mud flats and saltmarshes woven around this harbor inside a harbor.

Sprouting from a spongy honeycomb foundation of peat-like rich, organic soil from which grows salt-tolerant cordgrass, the saltmarsh is the rain forest of inland coastal regions, a veritable cornucopia of biodiversity. That organic bouquet is produced by the decomposition of organic matter, an estimated ten tons of which is generated annually per acre, making the saltmarsh one of the most productive ecosystems on earth. At Polpis Harbor, boaters, clam diggers, and estuarine wildlife co-exist in unique symbiosis.

Because this shallow harbor has distinct west and east lobes, the Native Americans that spoke Algonquian called it "Polpis," their word for "divided or branched harbor." The name was once spelled "Podpis," likely influenced by the Abnaki word for the harbor, *podebag*, which meant, "jutting of the water inland." The area was first called "Spotso Country" for an Indian chief named Spotso who lived nearby for about 40 years.

In the 1600s, farms sprouted all around the harbor, along with fulling mills to clean and prepare wool. Some industrious islanders built sea salt evaporator operations and also excavated peat from the saltmarsh to burn in stoves for heat.

What You'll See

Despite gradually encroaching development, the pristine quality of this inlet continues to draw scores of species of birds such as American oystercatchers, whimbrels, terns, ruddy turnstones, plovers, great blue and black-crowned night herons, Canada geese, sanderlings, stilts, and many sea ducks during the winter. So don't forget your binoculars for the birds and your camera for the glorious sunsets.

Walking through the upland meadows of this walk you'll discover a stand of holly trees and at the head of fields that lead down to the edges of Polpis Harbor. There, you'll marvel at precious views of Swain's Neck, Quaise Point, Pocomo Point, and parts of Medouie Creek.

When to Go

Any time is great for this walk. I like to visit Polpis after work during fall and winter, to catch the sunset. But I also love exploring the shoreline in the summer at dusk, in hopes that I'll see or hear some of the birds that live there. Of course low tide is the only time to experience the saltmarsh and its mud flats, because that's when their splendor is laid bare.

The Walk

Walking away (south) from the harbor on the landing's road, keep an eye out for a path marked by a green-and-white-capped post that reads "Nantucket Land Bank Public Sanctuary." Turn right (west) onto this path, which will lead you into 21 acres of land that the Land Bank bought in June 1996.

A stroll down this path will take you through a stand of holly trees, a peculiar sight when you are probably expecting rolling meadows

leading down to the harbor. The holly trees have outlasted the farm that once grew them, Holly Farm. To the north beyond the holly trees, as you meander down to the water, you'll discover that the Land Bank mows its meadows, making it easier for walkers to explore the property.

Once out in the meadow, you can wander down toward the harbor, keeping an eye out for a path that leads to a wood-chip-covered parking lot for boat trailers. Follow this path southeast to the parking area. To complete the loop, walk out onto the access road from the parking lot among the poplars and back out on the shore.

Getting There

Take Polpis Road to the start of Wauwinet Road. Right before Wauwinet Road on the north side of Polpis Road is Polpis Harbor Road. Go down this dirt track almost to water. The last left before the water leads to a spacious parking area. If traveling by bus, ride the 'Sconset via Polpis route and get off at Wauwinet Road. Just opposite the bus stop is the first entrance to Polpis Harbor. Cyclists should take the Polpis Road bike path to Wauwinet Road and then follow the same directions.

SCALLOP

POLPIS ROAD

MEDOUIE CREEK RD.

WAUWINET ROAD

EAT FIRE SPRING ROAD

.8 miles

Difficulty Rating: **
Dogs: Yes
Children: Yes

The Area

At dusk one hazy day just after the vernal equinox, I ventured out to the ocean end of Sesachacha Pond just as it was steadily disappearing into a misty blanket of fog. As the fog swirled around the pond, lifting and resettling over its shores, I caught fleeting glimpses of the pond's shores, a few dozen gulls and terns hanging out on its eastward edges, and the sun setting through the salty vapor.

If you love to explore shorelines, this walk around the ocean edges of Sesachacha Pond, where a narrow strip of sandy beach serves as a barrier between the two, will become one of your favorites. This area is a tranquil junction of many ecosystems that will keep you occupied for hours on countless late afternoons and early evenings, watching sea and marsh birds and poking around the ocean and pond shores.

This is an outing on which to use eyes more than legs. If it's warm enough, leave your shoes behind and pick your way down to the pond the way the rest of the animal world does. Don't worry about getting a chill from Sesachacha. Its water is tepid from spring through early fall. As early as late spring, even the ocean is warm enough for wading.

What You'll See

During the nesting season of the least tern, early spring through late summer, walk along the pond's edge from the beach and watch the terns dive into the water for minnows to feed to their chicks. In less than a foot of water, you can spot tiny hermit crabs scuttling across the shallow bottom and sparring with each other. On nearly windless days, it's relaxing to sit and listen to the miniature waves sloshing onto the beach.

You'll also find constantly changing sandbars that sometimes form a small inlet between the barrier beach and the pond. The sandbars, a residual effect of the temporary channel that the town opens between the pond and the ocean in spring and fall, form after the littoral drift of sand from north to south closes the opening, leaving a small, shallow cove in the pond.

In addition to letting blueback herring and American eels exchange environments twice a year for breeding purposes, this temporary breach in the barrier beach also rejuvenates the salinity and oxygen levels in the pond for the marine species that live in it.

To observe a pond opening is to witness how much sand the ocean currents and waves can throw around. Within one day, a six-foot wide ditch dug by an excavator can widen to a 100-foot wide canal; over the course of a week, that same beach channel will close in with sand and restore to its original condition, all from the natural movement of wind, currents, and waves.

A hike out to Sesachacha Pond on the spring and fall days when the town opens it to the ocean is a worthwhile adventure. While eels and herring pass each other in the salty waters of the fleeting waterway between sea and pond, gulls, terns, northern gannets, ospreys, and many other species of birds congregate on both shores and circle above. Just beyond the surf, striped bass swim close to the beach to feed on the herring and eels, and savvy fishermen angle for the bass.

When to Go

If you choose to explore the ocean side, try it at low tide. A great selection of rocks lures beachcombers in either direction. But leave what you find behind for other walkers to discover. Enjoy the rocks while you're there. It's exhilarating to stand calf-deep in the breaking waves and let the small, rounded stones wash over your feet. This is also a great place to watch a sunset, since you get to enjoy the colors playing on both ocean and pond. And if you can get up early enough, the sunrise here is spectacular. Try going about an hour before the sun sets or rises so you can watch the birds.

Because the beach is so exposed in late fall and winter, dress warmly, because the prevailing northeast winds can make this walk unbearable. Dogs are OK, but bring a leash in case the terns and plovers are nesting. And bring your children, because this is an easy walk with lots of natural sights for young eyes to see.

The Walk

All of these island wonders can be found about 100 yards from where you park your car or bike. Starting from the small parking area on the north side of the road, walk toward the ocean with the pond on your right. About 50 feet before the road turns to sand and continues through the dunes and out to the ocean, turn right toward the pond through a break in the split rail fence edging the road. Follow the short sand trail through a break in the dunes and out onto the beach. Now walk south down the beach keeping the pond on your right. Depending on when the pond was opened last, you may have to wade across the shallow mouth of the cut in the beach to reach the other side.

Getting There

Coming from either direction—Siasconset or town—turn onto Quidnet Road from Polpis Road. Near the end of Quidnet Road, turn right at the intersection. This road will take you down along the pond, ending with a beach trail into the dunes. You may park your bicycle or car along the right side of the road or in a parking area on the left side of the road. If you're using NRTA to reach the start of this walk, catch the 'Sconset via Polpis Road bus, get off at the Quidnet Road stop, and walk in to Quidnet from there, about 1.5 miles. Turn right at the intersection, following the road around to its end, and you'll find the pond.

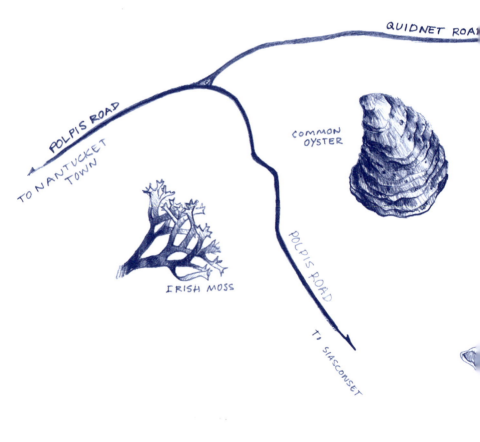

Difficulty Rating: ***
Dogs: Yes (leashed)
Children: Yes

3.2 miles

The Area

Can you imagine a place on Nantucket where, in the middle of the summer, there are only birds, waves, sun, and eelgrass tumbleweeds—and without hundreds of off-road vehicles?

If you can, you must be thinking about Smith's Point. Traditionally, from late spring through mid-August, this southwestern-most tip of Nantucket is closed to vehicle traffic for the sake of nesting tern species and, of course, the piping plover. Thankfully, for those who seek nearly deserted beaches for long beachcombing and wildlife-spotting jaunts, this remote sand spit that projects from the southwestern end of the island is a long slog through cool waters over mud flats, through a tern and gull rookery that will make you feel like you're in Alfred Hitchcock's *The Birds*. The allure of hiking past wind-blown beach grass magically sketching circles around their stalks in the sand, then out to the treacherous, pounding surf, where unforgiving undertows and rip tides wait to wash the unwary out sea, appeals to only a few of us. For the intrepid walker, this translates into all the more solitude for those who choose to explore this western extremity of Nantucket.

The orientation of Smith's Point makes it particularly vulnerable to hard-hitting southwesterly summer storms and hurricanes. Nantucket's sand spits and beaches are thought to have begun development roughly 5,000 years ago as a result of marine submergence of the land by a rising sea level related to the retreat of the glacier and erosion of previously deposited glacial rock debris.

What You'll See

Walking out to the remains of Smith's Point when it's closed to vehicle traffic offers not only tranquility, but also the chance to observe the results of the wind and water forces that are constantly building and then reclaiming this geologically battered peninsula. Like Great Point on Nantucket's northeastern tip, this part of Nantucket jabs a sandy finger out into sound and ocean. When you stand at the very tip of it, with the choppy rip churning just off the beach, you'll feel the vigor of the ocean's strength right at your feet. There is infinitely more to see at low tide. But remember that, while you can splash through and swim in the shallow water of the **harbor** side of Smith's Point if the mood hits you, there is a drop-off several yards out, marked by a darkening of the water. In any case, with no lifeguards on this beach, if you choose to swim here, you do it **at your own risk**.

Marine birds, including stilts, whimbrels, oystercatchers, ruddy turnstones, gulls, sandpipers, and, of course, plovers and terns, love the flats at low tide for the banquet of briny food provided either in a few inches of water or beneath the mud and sand. This smorgasbord of plankton, minnows, snails, hermit crabs, worms, and countless other marine goodies is exposed as the tide lowers. The shore birds will work these flats all day long, and you can spend hours watching them pick through the mud and shallow water before they rest and then bathe.

When to Go

Because of the diversity of birds you'll see on Smith's Point, this walk is enjoyable all year long. From fall through early spring, it's delightful to walk around the inlet on the harbor side of Smith's Point and out to the sand spit, formerly Esther's Island, to just east of the last house on the

point. Try this walk on windless, sunny days in winter and look for a spot on the beach against the dunes where you can doze off. In fall and winter, when you won't disturb the inhabitants of the three houses, you can enjoy a good loop walk all the way around the attached Esther's Island, out to Smith's Point, and back to your vehicle.

Remember, though, that during spring and summer, the harbor side of the inlet is a well-protected gull nesting area that you should avoid. If you doubt my advice, try to approach it: the gulls will dive-bomb you from all directions to protect their young.

The Walk

Begin at the Smith's Point beach shack on Massachusetts Avenue in Madaket, keeping the harbor on your right, and walk south down Massachusetts Avenue. You'll know you're moving in the right direction if you soon pass on the right a house with a quarterboard on its gable end that reads "Crooked House." If you end up at a boat landing, you went the wrong direction. Once you've found your way to the ocean end of Massachusetts Avenue—basically, when the hard sand road turns to loose sand and runs up through a dune—cross the dune and follow the sand road to the first proper right (northwest) turn through the dunes onto the beach along Madaket Harbor.

As you beach-comb your way across mudflats and sand, you'll eventually encounter a narrow but deep inlet. If you don't mind schlepping your rods and gear across the flats, this inlet is sometimes full of fish. This inlet was formed when Hurricane Esther hit the waters off Madaket with late summer winds of up to 110 knots on September 21, 1961, isolating part of Smith's Point from the main island. This temporary cay was christened Esther's Island after the storm that created it. Working gradually, but not always diligently, the ocean reconnected Esther's Island to Smith's Point in 1988. The inlet was thus formed on the north side of Smith's Point, and Madaket Harbor was protected from the ocean once more. To complete the walk, just stroll past the inlet, keeping it to your right, and walk through the dunes away from Madaket Harbor and toward the sound of the ocean, taking care not to step directly on the beach grass, which dies when its stalks are broken. If the terns and plovers are nesting, then you should have the beach to yourself.

If you need to cool off during your summer walk, for safety's sake, swimming on the ocean side of Smith's Point isn't recommended, because the currents, rip tides, and undertows around Smith's Point are no joke. You can easily get pulled out into the churning water and drown. If you want to take a dip, swim in Madaket Harbor, but never alone.

Getting There

To reach Massachusetts Avenue in Madaket by auto or by bicycle, travel west on Madaket Road from the intersection of New Lane, Upper Main Street, and Quaker Road. At the end of Madaket Road, turn right onto Ames Avenue, cross a wooden bridge, and follow the dirt road as it bends left and then right again. This will eventually end at Massachusetts Avenue, which runs north-south. At this intersection, you'll see, at the edge of the dunes just ahead to the left, the shack from which the town sells beach-driving stickers and dispenses beach-driving advice. If the few parking spaces on the west side of the road are full, you can leave your car further ahead, at the bottom of the dune that leads out to Smith's Point. There is also parking at north end of Massachusetts Avenue, near the pier that overlooks Hither Creek and at the end of Madaket Road, just before Ames Avenue.

If you're traveling by bus, take NRTA's Madaket route from town all the way to its last stop in front of the Westender Restaurant, then walk to the end of the road and pick up the driving directions at the turn onto Ames Avenue.

Moors and Meadows

This island must look exactly like a prairie, except that the view in clear weather is bounded by the sea.
— Henry David Thoreau on Nantucket

85 + **Bald Spot Behind My House (Radar Hill)**

91 + **Head of the Plains**

97 + **Madequecham Valley**

103 + **Pout Ponds**

111 + **Sanford Farm**

125 + **Tupancy Links**

Bald Spot Behind My House (Radar Hill)

.6 miles

Difficulty Rating: *
Dogs: Yes
Children: Yes

The Area

The relative flatness of Nantucket means that, unfortunately, most of the island's scenic vistas are visible only from the widow's walks on the tops of private homes. For the walker, that leaves only a handful of high spots to choose from. Of these, the one you should find the most rewarding is a little nub off Polpis Road locally known as Radar Hill.

From its crest you can see most of town and Nantucket Harbor, the Cliff, almost all of Coatue, Coskata Pond and its woods, Pocomo Point, Polpis Harbor, all of the Galls and Great Point, Sankaty Head and its lighthouse, Siasconset, and the moors between Polpis Road and Milestone Road. You'll be amazed at how quickly and effortlessly you can take in a large chunk of Nantucket's land mass, its harbor, and Nantucket Sound.

You'll be walking in the part of the island called the Shawaukemo Hills, popularly shortened to Shawkemo. Shawaukemo, a section of the island west of Quaise Point, may have been the site of an Indian settlement. The hills themselves run from the North Pasture Lane hill on down to just northwest of the Pout Ponds. Their name is believed to be linked to the Algonquian word for "great house," *k'chekomuck*, and as one of the island's few high spots, the hill gives one the feeling of standing on the widow's walk of a tall house in town, scanning the ocean for incoming whaling ships.

When to Go

After walking this one in every month of the year—because the view is so spectacular—all I can say about which season is best for hiking up Radar Hill is that you shouldn't miss one of them. It doesn't matter. Nantucket is beautiful spring, summer, fall, and winter.

The rewards for this loop are immediate and completely satisfying because you can get the view anytime with minimal effort. You should know that Radar Hill is a favorite local hangout for Nantucket's younger set.

The Walk

From the parking area next to the bike path, a dirt road leads into the moors. Follow it south-southeast, ignoring the first left turn (the end of this loop) that appears after about 100 yards. Do take the second left and follow that road up to the top of the hill.

For the return, either go back down the hill the way you came or walk east down a gradual decline. If you choose the latter, shortly after you descend into the brush, take a hard left that will guide you back in the direction from which you came. Follow the dirt road running along the north slope of Radar Hill as it opens up to reveal a deep ravine and a grassy meadow spreading out to the east. When this trail forms a T-intersection with the path on which you started, turn right and walk out to the bike path and Polpis Road.

Getting There

From the start of Polpis Road just before Island Lumber, go 1.5 miles to the turn for North Pasture Lane on the south side of Polpis Road. From North Pasture Lane, go about three tenths of a mile and just after #116 Polpis Road, look for a right turn down an asphalt apron between a grove of cedar trees lined on either side with concrete posts. Cross the bike path and park in one of the two spots next to the path. If you're traveling from Wauwinet and Quidnet, the turn is the next left after #127 Polpis Road.

Those traveling by bicycle should follow the Polpis Road bike path from Milestone Road out past the turn for North Pasture Lane, which is marked with two white posts bearing that name. Take the next right. You can also take the NRTA's 'Sconset Route via Polpis Road bus to the North Pasture Lane stop, then walk east and take the next right.

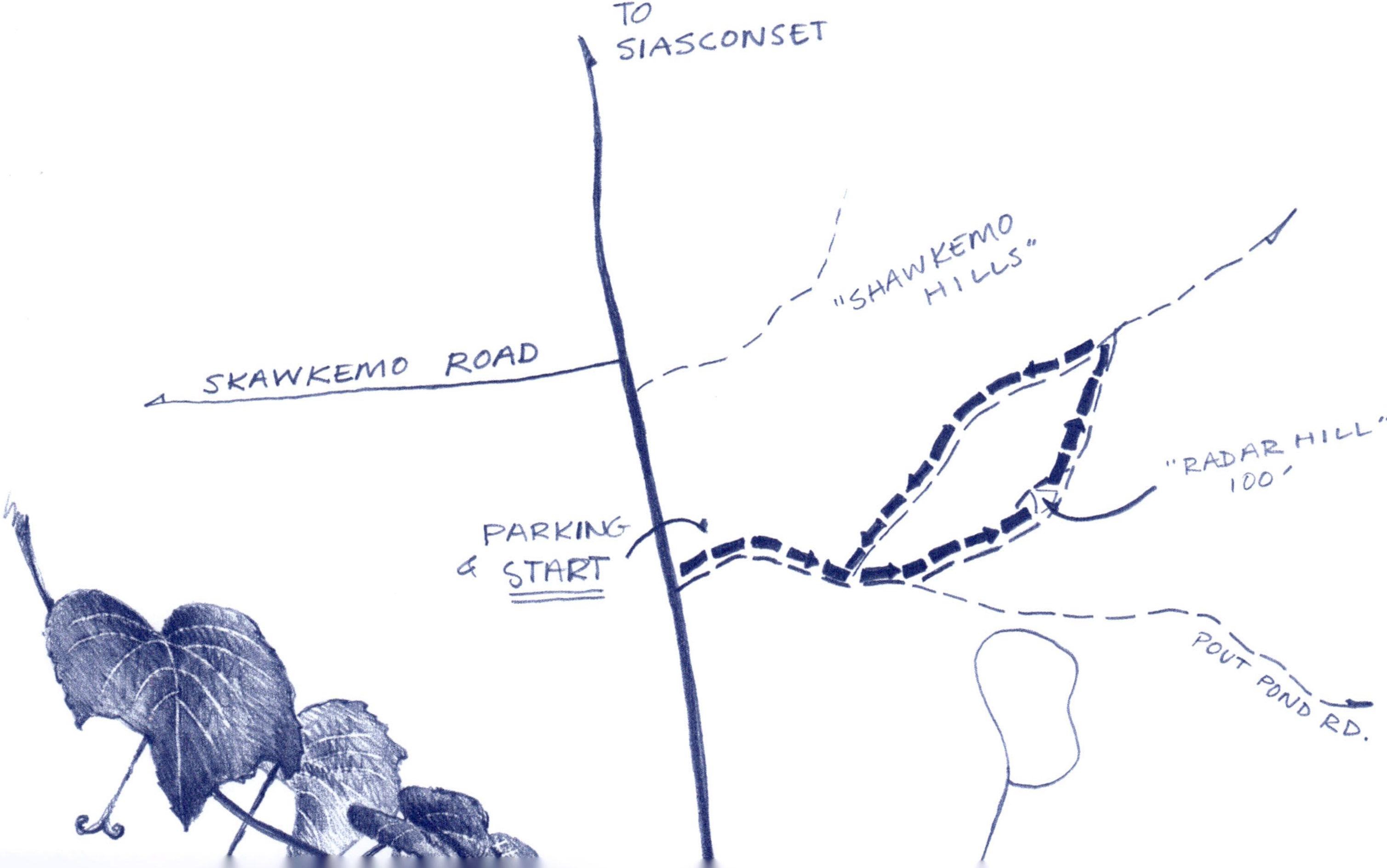

Bald Spot Behind My House (Radar Hill)

To Siasconset

- Skawkemo Road
- "Shawkemo Hills"
- "Radar Hill" 100'
- Pout Pond Rd.
- Parking & Start

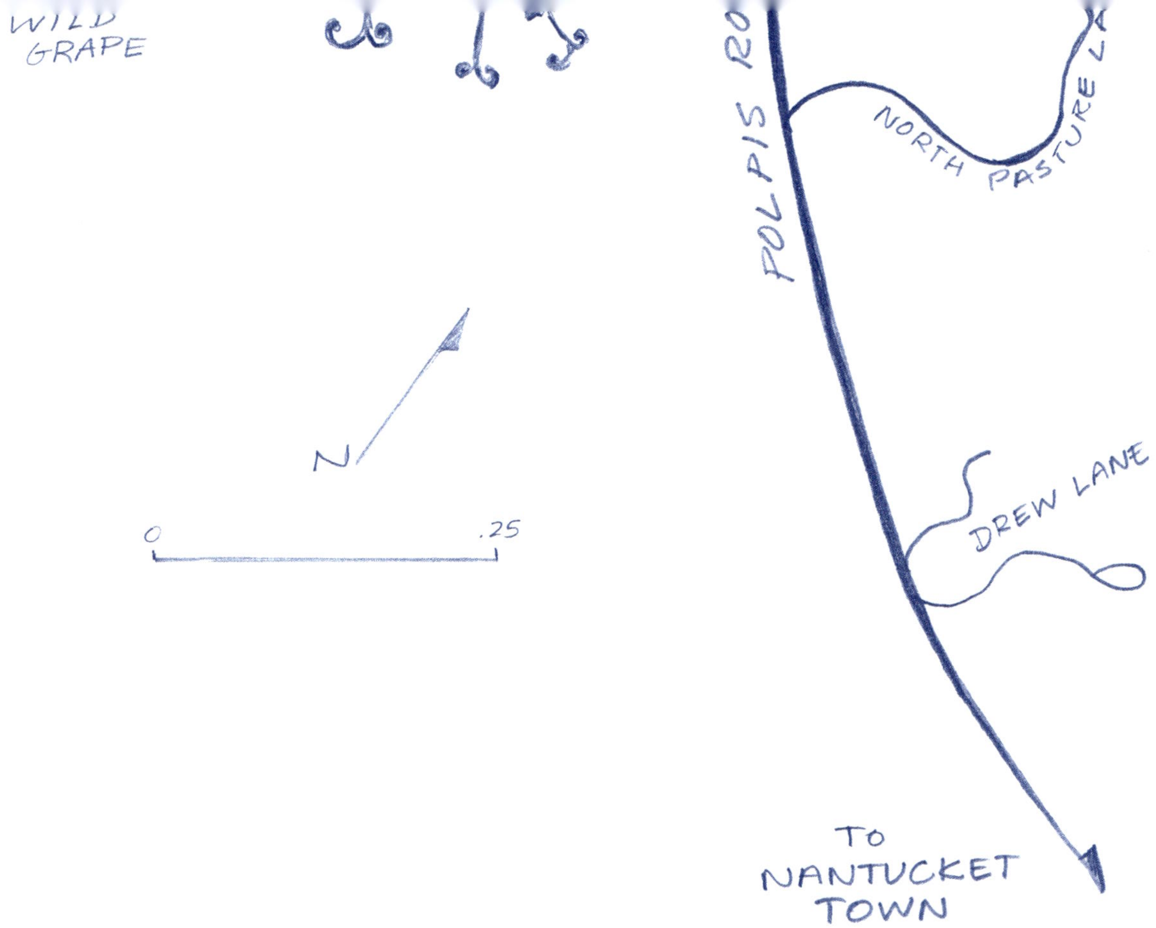

NORTH PASTURE LN

POLPIS RD

DREW LANE

TO NANTUCKET TOWN

WILD GRAPE

N

0 .25

+ WALKING NANTUCKET • BALD SPOT BEHIND MY HOUSE (RADAR HILL)

Head of the Plains

Difficulty Rating: **
Dogs: Yes
Children: Yes

2.3 miles

The Area

When I want to feel the physical creation of Nantucket, to walk through the fruits of its geologically fortunate past, I go to the Head of the Plains on the southeast side of Madaket. Comprised of 800 acres of sandplain grasslands, Head of the Plains is owned by three different entities: the Nantucket Conservation Foundation (roughly 433 acres), the Nantucket Islands Land Bank, and the U.S. Government.

Easily some of the most beautiful open land on the island, Head of the Plains is the low-lying flat land that the glacier left behind, called, in geological terms, an outwash plain. As the glacier retreated, its trailing meltwater deposited sand, gravel, and other detritus in its smoothing wake. An ecosystem known as sandplain grassland took hold in the nutrient-rich seaside soils.

Sandplain grasslands are now endangered. They are so rare today that roughly 90 percent of earth's remaining sandplain grasslands—including Head of the Plains—are found on Nantucket and Tuckernuck islands and the island of Martha's Vineyard. Nantucket's first settlers let sheep loose on Nantucket's open lands, in the start of an industry that ultimately swelled to a collective herd in the tens of thousands. The sheep kept the island's larger native woody plants like scrub oak and pitch pine from establishing themselves. Instead, the prairie-like plants flourished. Now, in the absence of sheep, wind and salt spray—to a limited degree—keep the invasive larger plants from completely taking over the plains.

What You'll See

Fortunately for this splendid landscape, the only growth taller than the low plants that the Head of the Plains has seen in this century are a sprinkling of houses toward the south end of Long Pond, a radio tower, and houses lining the east side of Hummock Pond in the distance.

Thousands of years after the glacier departed, the sandplain grasslands continues to thrive on Nantucket with a miniature ecosystem of low, rare grasses, wildflowers, and shrubs, including bearberry, with oval, shiny leaves and cranberry-sized berries; false heather, also called poverty grass, which produces small yellow flowers in spring; and a lichen called alpine reindeer moss. Rare and endangered plant species, such as St. Andrew's cross, broom crowberry, sandplain blue-eyed grass, bushy rockrose, and sandplain flax, proliferate there as well.

Of course, you will see red-tailed hawks soaring above you, along with northern harriers hovering low over the brush in search of rodents. Smaller birds, like song sparrows, gray catbirds, rufous-sided towees, and swallows, also thrive on these open lands.

When to Go

I like being out on this island plain when the fog is slowly rolling in at dusk, so I can watch the northern harriers swooping low over the brush, disappearing and reappearing in the fog. A visitor to this area can easily lose sight of all man-made intrusions and get lost in Nantucket's geological genesis. The thunderous crashing of the ocean's waves on the beach completes the experience.

Because the mosaic of the sandplain grasslands changes dramatically with the seasons, you'll find that you'll want to experience these walks in winter, spring, summer, and fall. When you go, bring your children and your

dogs, if leashed, but don't forget to take away with you all your trash—and any more you have room to carry. This sweeping landscape remains the way is it because of those who care deeply for it.

The Walk

From the parking area next to Massasoit Bridge, ignore the left turn that runs along the parking lot and walk straight along the wide dirt road which heads southeast, for roughly a quarter of a mile. Upon reaching a fork in the road, take the left and walk down a gradual descent. Shortly after the fork, this wide track, known as Massasoit Road, becomes two separate dirt roads running tightly parallel to each other. Take your pick and walk along one of these roads until you reach the ocean.

As you walk along, you will see various other roads that cut into the plains. Exploration of these paths is up to you, your compass, and your map of the island. Remember that it's almost impossible to get completely lost on the island and that, to find your way back to the end of this walk, you just retrace your steps.

Getting There

Take Madaket Road or its bike path from their beginning at Caton Circle almost to Madaket village and turn left onto South Cambridge Street, heading southeast. To get there without your own vehicle, hop on NRTA's Madaket Route bus and get off at the Cambridge Street stop.

Travel directly down South Cambridge Street, ignoring all turns. Just after you sight Midland Avenue on the right, cross Massasoit Bridge, the narrow wooden bridge with white railings. If you brought a car or bike, turn left just after the bridge and park in the grassy area along Long Pond, marked by a gate that reads, "Nantucket Islands Land Bank Commission." This parking area is four-tenths of a mile from Madaket Road—about a 10-minute walk.

From the parking area, walk back out to the dirt track called Massasoit Road at the near end of the bridge and walk left, roughly southeast, to the fork in the road.

Madequecham Valley

1.2 miles

Difficulty Rating: *
Dogs: Yes
Children: Yes

The Area

There's short loop out around Madequecham Valley just east of Nantucket Memorial Airport that's near the beach and away from the more crowded walking trails on the island. This gradually disappearing pond is now more mud and cattails than water, but I imagine it was much like my childhood swimming hole, a shallow pond with a muddy bottom, dotted with lily pads at one end and sporting a manmade sand beach at the other. The cool water of this pond during sweltering summers was only half the fun: the painted turtles, frogs, tadpoles, and red-winged blackbirds got equal attention from me.

The late Dr. Wes Tiffney, former director of the University of Massachusetts Field Station, said that the pond was created as the island-forming glacier began its retreat, some 15,000 years ago, when summer temperatures warmed enough to cause melting of the glacial ice front, called moraine. Sheets of meltwater flowed southward toward the ocean, then miles beyond where it lies today. Fine loads of silt and clay were carried to the ocean and today form the sea floor.

The flow of the meltwater was strong enough to carry heavier loads of sand, gravel, and stones hundreds of feet, sometimes a few miles. The further away from its source the meltwater got, the weaker the flow became and the heavier the loads of sand and gravel that were dropped, creating what is now Nantucket's outwash plain. The outwash plain is relatively flat and generally spans the southern half of the island.

Later in the glacial retreat, at the hands of increasingly warmer temperatures, the floodwaters of the melting ice moved quickly enough to scour out valleys from the accumulated sand and gravel.

Madequecham, Toupshue, and Forked Pond valleys once contained shoreline ponds that extended at least another quarter of a mile beyond the island's southern shores. But over the years, erosion by wind and water has rolled back the land, advancing the beach inland, and the stormwash has elevated the bottom of each valley above the water table. Gradually, the ponds disappeared, leaving dry valleys for you to walk through. The same metamorphosis is slowly happening to Miacomet Pond, Hummock Pond, Clark Cove, and Long Pond.

What You'll See

The last vestiges of pond vegetation in Madequecham Valley, cattails, can be seen growing about 100 yards back from the beach; they are home to red-winged blackbirds. The low areas sometimes contain standing water during the spring months. Be on the lookout for small birds, the occasional white-tailed deer bounding across the low plants, northern harriers sweeping the valley for rabbits and mice, and several wild species of lilies.

Also, walk in front of the pond with the ocean at your back and notice how the sand moves inland toward the pond like a plant-suffocating lava flow. Fall and winter storms push the sand up over the dunes and into the inland vegetation.

When to Go

Because of the diversity of plant and animal life in this area, I recommend taking this walk all year long to see the changes in color of the vegetation in the valley along with the species. As ponds like these gradually dry up into a

partial wetland, eventually becoming dry land, the plant and animal life changes with it.

About an hour before sunset, from spring through late summer, is when the wildlife comes out and the fading light plays on the ocean and moors around the pond. In fall, it's a real treat to experience the foliage, subtle as it is, and in winter to see snow all over the land.

The Walk

From the parking area, walk back out the way you came, with the ocean now at your back. After the curves and undulations of the dirt road cease, take the first right you come to and then the next right and follow that dirt road down into the valley so that you're pointed toward the ocean. You're now standing where the pond used to be, one of the lowest parts of the island. Continue on southeast until you reach a road that heads back toward the sea.

Stay on this road, ignoring all turns, and it will lead you right to the beach, another distraction that may add time to your walking schedule. Once on the beach, walk west a short distance to a sand path that becomes a wood chip trail running up the bluff to the parking lot. You might find a few bass and bluefish fishers working the surf when you go, but it's not uncommon to take this walk, even in summer, and not see another person or vehicle.

Getting There

Find New South Road off the Milestone Road—the nearest NRTA bus stop, Nobadeer Farm Road on the 'Sconset/Town Route, is about a half mile from this road. Travel to the dirt end of New South Road and take the middle prong of a three-way fork, a long, washboard-surfaced road. You'll know that you're on the right dirt track if the airport's black chain-link fence is immediately on your right. Follow this road as it dips and rises and rolls east and west several times. When you can see the ocean ahead of you, and just before the road turns sharply to the right and continues west still paralleling the airport fence, take a left that will drop you down a sand road and then up to a dirt parking lot on a bluff owned and maintained by the Land Bank.

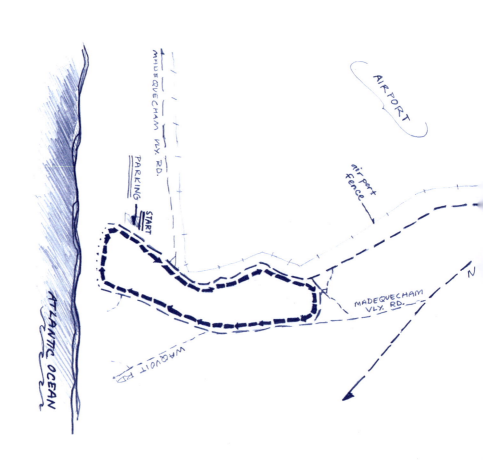

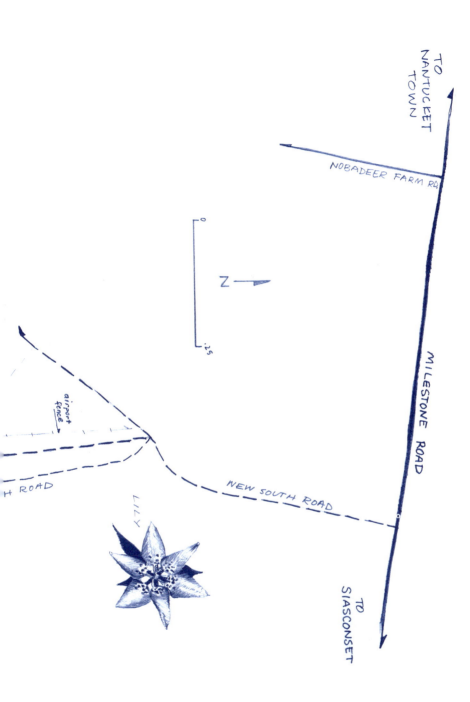

Pout Ponds

2.5 miles

Difficulty Rating: ***
Dogs: Yes
Children: Yes

The Area

When Nantucket residents approved a $25 million bond at the 1997 Annual Town Meeting, the first parcel the Land Bank acquired was the Rhoates property off Polpis Road. Just southwest of this property are the Pout Ponds.

I had heard of the Pout (pronounced "poot") Ponds from an island friend, and though I'd seen them from the air dozens of times, I could never locate them on any of my mountain biking or walking trips out into the moors. Nantucket is peppered with kettle holes like the Pout Ponds, but this pair can be tough to locate without directions. The ponds, fed only by rainwater, are deep in Nantucket's interior, the area islanders refer to as the moors.

The Shawkemo Hills area, an undulating landscape of low brush, scrub oak, and pitch pine, was once simple grasslands where Nantucket's founders grazed their sheep. The sheep's appetite prevented dominant woody plants from overgrowing the land. But when the whaling industry took hold on Nantucket, residents put down their shears and picked up harpoons. The resulting maze of vegetation is what you'll see as you explore the moors.

What You'll See

At the start of this walk, you'll have the opportunity to learn to spot the common coastal heathland plants that you will see throughout this walk. Bearberry, for example, is the plentiful sub-shrub of the moors. Growing low on the ground, it often appears in large patches, filling in bare spots. On the left several feet from the start of this walk is a large patch of bearberry. Its bell-shaped white and pink flowers can be seen in April and May, its fruit from June into the fall. Also growing near the start of this walk is little bluestem grass that grows up to two feet high and covers much of the moors with its colorful blossoms each season.

Huckleberry and bayberry grow in this area as well. Huckleberry is similar to low bush blueberry, but it is more prolific in the central moors. Its closely formed, sweeping strands of growth provide a spectacular display of red to maroon in the fall. In the summer, the foliage and berries offer food and shelter to birds and small mammals. Bayberry is another dominant shrub common to the moors. From its light gray twigs extend glossy green leaves that give off the same aroma as their waxy blue-gray berries, which are often used to scent candles. You will also see pitch pine and scrub oak on this walk. As you explore the Shawkemo Hills, you will see how pervasive each of these heathland plants is.

When you reach the Pout Ponds, the vegetation in and around them is worth attention. From the head of the first pond, you'll be able to see variegated rings of vegetation that grow away from the pond. The upland outer ring is dominated by scrub oak with some high bush blueberry and winterberry. Closer to the pond is a ring of grasses and goldenrod. Closer still, a ring of rush and sedge is sprinkled with sphagnum moss. And in the center of the pond, a stand of tussock sedge grows. The water level in the Pout Ponds fluctuates, disqualifying it as a wet meadow—a seasonal pond that fills with water in spring and fall and is usually bare ground in

summer and winter. Sometimes the water rises as high as the edge of the tree line; other times, particularly during late summer, surface water may not even reach the ring of rush and sedge.

The second pond has the same concentric circles of upland and wetland plants, primarily rush and tussock sedge. Study the north end of the pond and notice how it is filling in with plants. As low water levels expose the pond bottom, wetland vegetation gradually gains a foothold. Over many years, the leaf and stalk litter of this migrant vegetation builds up the bottom of the pond, enabling creeping encroachment into the pond.

The brush overhanging the shores of these ponds provides excellent cover for several types of ducks and for thirsty deer. On occasion, I've spooked least bitterns, green herons, great blue herons, great egrets, little egrets, mallards, and Canada Geese during their "hidden" fishing jaunts. You can avoid scaring off wildlife by walking into the wind.

On the moors around these ponds, you'll most certainly see northern harriers, red-tailed hawks, towees, catbirds, and many other smaller birds. Whitetail deer can be seen if you're quiet and observant.

When to Go

All of the high spots on this route are marvelous places for sunsets and stargazing. During the day, pick any time and you won't be disappointed. An early morning walk means more wildlife and fewer people. An evening stroll in the gathering fog is my favorite, because you can see wonderful sunsets through the fog.

You shouldn't pass up this walk during the fall foliage season, and a hike here during or just after a snowstorm is an indescribable island experience.

I do avoid going out in the moors during the hotter days of summer, usually in July and August.

The Walk

Beginning at the edge of the Polpis Road bike path, the Pout Ponds walk runs south up a dirt road into the moors. Take the first left off of the dirt road you're walking on. This road will lead you up to a great view of a ravine. Looking down into this typically mountainous feature, you'll be amazed at the steepness of the slope and at the miniature valley below that runs away to the east. Leaving the ravine behind you, follow the dirt road up into a thicket. Looking north from this entrance back into the low trees, you'll get another great view of this valley, part of the Shawkemo Hills area. Walk southeast along the road until you can see, off to the right, several posts blocking vehicles from a small rise beyond. Ascend this rise via the trail, and you'll get a sweeping view of the moors to the southeast.

Scan the eastern horizon, just west of Altar Rock, and you'll glimpse a white structure, something like a bowling pin, that airplanes use for navigation. Southeast of this man-made landmark is the silvery water tower out in Siasconset. During the fall, the Pout Ponds should be visible directly south of this hill. Walk south down the hill and over a second little hump, ignoring the trail that diverges to the left. If you pass between two wooden posts, you're on the right trail. You're now standing at the bottom of what some islanders call the Devil's Punch Bowl, named for the explosion of red fall foliage that appears in autumn.

Continue south on this road until you reach an intersection. This crossroad is Pout Pond Road. Once across it, you'll see the first pond to your left. This pair of ponds is called both Foot Ponds, because from the air they look like a pair of footprints, and Pout Ponds, because early fishermen used to catch in them a species of fish called hornpout. Walk on a little further and bear left and you'll be at the head of the first pond, or continue on about 100 yards and you'll come to the second pond on your right.

When you're ready to resume the walk, retrace your steps to the intersection of Pout Pond Road. Instead of crossing the road this time, turn left onto Pout Pond Road and head west. Stay on this road as it slowly rises and curves to the right, past a dense stand of black tupelo

trees on the right. On the right of the road, see if you can spot a fern-like plant with a woody stem. The leaves of this plant, called sweet fern, have a pleasantly fresh smell and are thought to have been placed in pillows of yore to enhance sweet dreams. But please don't pick the leaves of this fern. Leave the plants intact for their continued survival and for others to enjoy. Further along the road, on the right, is a low grassy area with a distinctive swath of rush signifying a wet or moist section of field. At the top of the rise, just before another stand of tupelo, look to the left. The sweeping, open, grassy area gives a sense of how the moors looked when sheep grazed island-wide. Here, Nantucket's ubiquitous scrub oaks are just starting to grow in.

Shortly after the tupelo grove, take the next right and walk north up a hill toward a group of houses on North Pasture Lane. Ignore all the right turns and follow this road as it narrows to a bike trail that tunnels through the scrub oaks. When you crest the hill, passing a short section of split rail fence on the left while walking through deep sand, you're almost back to Polpis Road. Continue to follow the bike trail as it gradually widens into a dirt road.

Getting There

From the start of Polpis Road just before Island Lumber, go 1.5 miles to the turn for North Pasture Lane on the south side of Polpis Road. From North Pasture Lane, go about three tenths of a mile and just after #116 Polpis Road, look for a right turn down an asphalt apron between a grove of cedar trees lined on either side with concrete posts. Cross the bike path and park in one of the two spots next to the path. If you're traveling from Wauwinet and Quidnet, the turn is the next left after #127 Polpis Road

Those traveling by bicycle should follow the Polpis Road bike path from Milestone Road out past the turn for North Pasture Lane, which is marked with two white posts bearing that name. Take the next right. You can also take the NRTA's 'Sconset Route via Polpis Road bus to the North Pasture Lane stop, then walk east and take the next right.

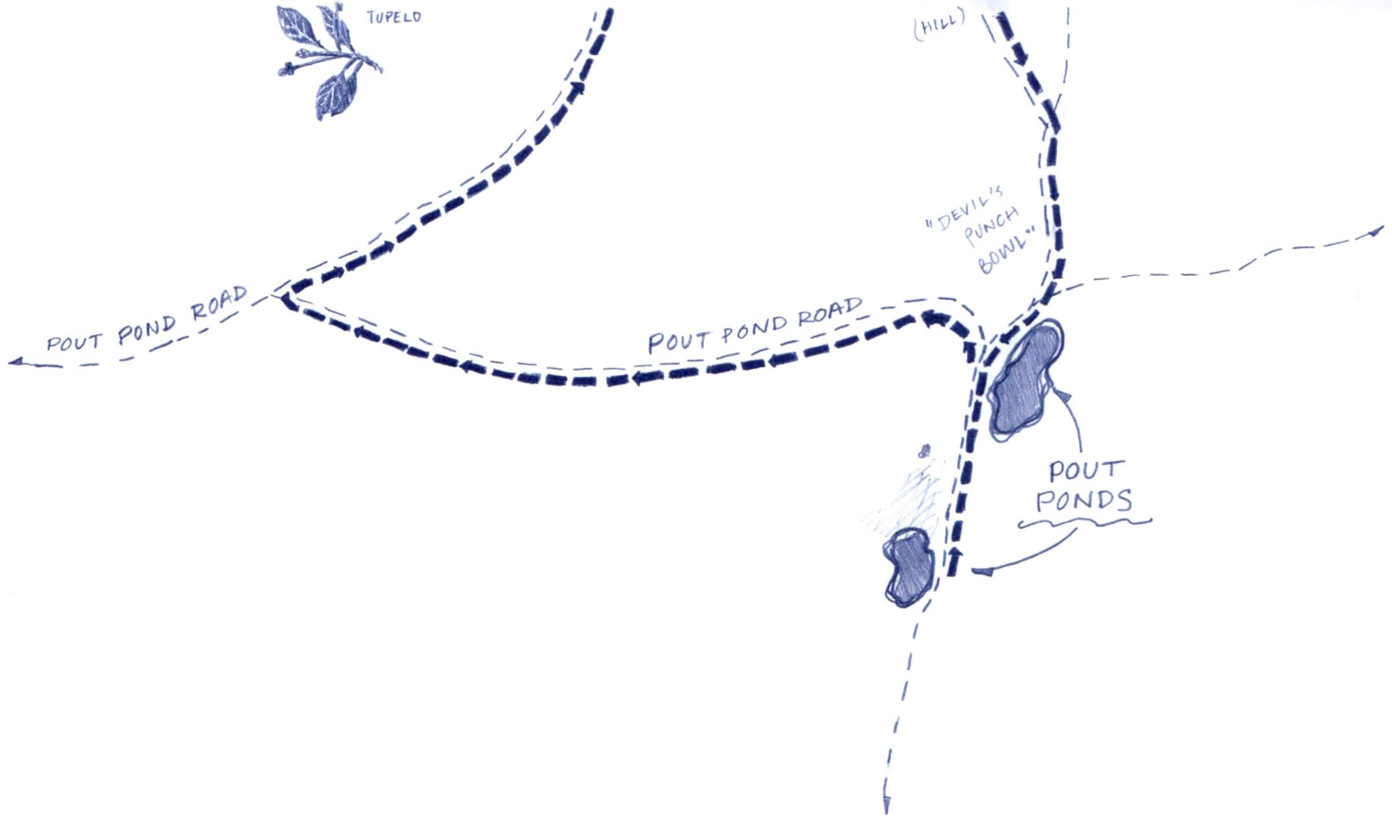

108 • WALKING NANTUCKET • POUT PONDS

POUT POND ROAD

POUT POND ROAD

TUPELO

"DEVIL'S PUNCH BOWL"

(HILL)

POUT PONDS

The Area

The crown jewel of the Nantucket Conservation Foundation's 8,700 acres of preserved open space is the 767.5-acre Sanford Farm property off Madaket Road. For first-time explorers of this island, the trails on the Sanford Farm property are a great introduction to Nantucket's wilderness. This extraordinary parcel of rolling fields, thickets, low forests, marshlands, sandplain grasslands, and ponds offers miles and miles of trails for outdoor enthusiasts to explore. In just one outing through the Woods and Ram Pasture and along Hummock Pond, Clark Cove, and Head of the Hummock sections of this property, you pass through almost all of the ecosystems found on Nantucket.

The ocean end of the property is known as Ram Pasture and was originally inhabited by Native Americans ruled by a chief named Nanahuma. It first fell into English hands when the chief sold the land for 25 pounds in 1664, just five years after 27 English settlers from the mainland founded Sherburne, Nantucket's first incorporated town, on the shores of what is now Capaum Pond, then an open harbor. Farms that were part of that first town operated on and around the land now called Sanford Farm.

Since these settlers were primarily farmers, and Nantucket of the 17th century almost completely grasslands, sheep farming evolved into the island's first industry. Lacking the time and energy to erect fences to cordon off each farmer's land, Nantucket's settlers agreed to share the land on which their collective herd grazed. These lands came to be called "sheep commons shares" because the so-called commons were shared by all the sheep farmers for the greater good of the young island community.

Ram Pasture got its name from the sheep farming practice of grazing the rams in this pasture away from the ewes so that they wouldn't risk rearing their lambs during the winter.

After whaling replaced the island sheep industry and then met its own demise, the agrarian use of the lands of Sanford Farm was expanded into dairy farming until the early 1920s. Anne W. Sanford—the last owner of the property, who purchased the land from its last farmer, Randolph Swain—helped found the Nantucket Conservation Foundation, and in 1985, the late Mrs. Sanford's estate sold 133.5 acres to the Foundation and 166.5 acres to the Nantucket Islands Land Bank, marking a first-time island conservation collaborative between the year-old Land Bank and the Foundation. The balance of the current acreage of the property—467.5 acres including the Woods and Ram Pasture—had been purchased by the Foundation in 1971 with money donated by 250 of its members. To honor her gift, the Nantucket Conservation Foundation thought it apropos that all 767.5 acres be named after the venerable Anne W. Sanford.

Finding Your Own Path

As noted before, it is impossible to write about every walking path on the island. What *Walking Nantucket* offers are samples of the island wild that can spur you to make your own discoveries.

On the Sanford Farm property, many mown cuts snake away from the primary trails into the brush and out onto protected meadows not visible from the main track. Exploration of all of these little trails at your leisure will expand your knowledge and appreciation of the Sanford Farm property. But don't stray from them. There are literally hundreds of

miles of deer trails crisscrossing the island. Leave these trails to the deer, rabbits, and other animals that need cover. Stay on clearly marked, obvious trails for humans.

What You'll See

Along the trails of Sanford Farm are 26 information posts that tell visitors what they're seeing and offer historical tidbits. Each post also notes distances to various points on the property. All in all, the seven miles of trails on the Sanford Farm property form an introductory course in experiencing Nantucket on foot. The paths are wide and well marked, there is plenty of parking just off Madaket Road, and maps are available at the start of the walk, as well as at the Foundation's office at 118 Cliff Road.

However, a word of advice to those seeking solitude just outside of town: in relative terms, Sanford Farm is the Central Park of Nantucket. Unless you prefer early, early morning walks or nighttime strolls, you're bound to encounter plenty of passive traffic, including walkers, runners, mountain bikers, and horseback riders. Sanford Farm is the Foundation's most popular, and therefore most utilized, property. On the other hand, if you like to socialize along the way and love sharing your walking experience with others, you'll be at home on these walks.

What you see on this property is as much up to you as it is up to the time of year and day you choose to walk, along with your choice of which part of Sanford Farm you walk through, but many of the sights and views of this property are a constant. If you hike out to the barn, you'll notice that it's architecturally pleasing on the outside, with its little cupola on top, but the barn is really a maintenance shed perched on a rise about 50 feet above sea level. Sweeping views of the Atlantic Ocean stretch out before you along Nantucket's South Shore.

Down to the left (southeast), running north to south, is Hummock Pond. The wide path you see in the direction of the pond once led to a bridge that crossed the narrowest section of the pond and allowed sheep farmers to herd their rams over to Ram Pasture. Ram Pasture is the open field due south, lying between the barn and the ocean.

The body of water southwest of the vantage point of the barn is Clark Cove, which was once part of Hummock Pond until it was separated by the gigantic storm surge created by the Blizzard of 1978. While the worst blizzard in decades was dumping several feet of snow on the mainland, its winds created waves that chewed deep into the sand at the west end of Cisco Beach, where the pond took its bend to the northwest, and temporarily opened the pond to the ocean then closed it off with sand, thus forming two separate ponds. Imagine the ferocity of a storm that could re-shape that much beach in such a short time.

In one or two spots along the shores of both ponds are telephone poles stripped of their crossbars and insulators. Planted in the muck of the ponds, these poles now serve as platforms for osprey nests. The nests are always active, and in spring, avid birders remain on the lookout for the first osprey sighting of the new season. Massive nests of tree limbs and cattails are the perfect high spots from which adult, and sometimes, young ospreys, launch their pond-fishing sorties. If you like diving birds, also be on the lookout for kingfishers diving in the pond in spring through summer, and for terns and northern gannets diving for fish just off the beach in spring through summer, and again in winter. Great blue herons, black-crowned night herons, great egrets, and little egrets can be seen scouring the edges of the ponds for fish and frogs.

Out on Ram Pasture and the lands west of Clark Cove, notice the openness of the sandplain grassland and the vibrant colors of grasses, wildflowers, sky, pond, and ocean. Virtually treeless and without structures, this habitat once extended all along the South Shore outwash plain, where glacial meltwater deposited sediments of mud, clay, sand, silt, and pebbles. Winds laden with salt-spray stunt the growth of trees whose limbs are swept northward by prevailing southwest winds. Tribes of Wampanoag Indians used fire to clear the land for hunting, and colonists grazed sheep in the grasslands. Rare plant species, such as little

bluestem grass, Pennsylvania sedge, poverty grass, bushy rockrose, sandplain blue-eyed grass, asters, and goldenrods, prevail on this low seashore landscape.

When to Go

Like Central Park, Sanford Farm is still open to the walking, running, jogging, and cycling public when the mercury drops. It's a safe bet that the property sees nearly as much use in the colder months as it does in spring and summer. So in deciding when to walk these extraordinary acres, choose days during each month of the year.

Most people who exercise outdoors love this part of the island for its proximity to the ocean and salt ponds, and the amazing views of both from several knolls along the route. Across the four seasons, a visitor to Sanford Farm is likely to find returning migratory birds building nests among the flowers and new leaves in the spring; nesting least terns and piping plovers near warm ocean waters in the summer; fall foliage and hurricane waves in autumn; and the rare sight of snow covering the open lands and beaches in winter, with sea ducks and gulls playing on the waves.

Sanford Farm is a year-round good walking spot because many of its trails are sheltered from the cold winds of fall and winter by brush and low trees. And in the summer, its trails all lead down to the beach.

A note about Barrett Farm Road before you start: this road is a favorite route for mountain bikers who love to ride their titanium steeds through mud and puddles. What that means to a walker is waterproof boots during spring and fall. Sometimes the puddles are deep enough to cover the entire road, but during most of the summer, they amount to little more than shallow pools of mud and or muddy water that you can easily walk around.

The Walks

Main Trail to the Barn

Length: 3.2 miles
Difficulty Rating: ****
Dogs: Yes
Children: Yes

The bucolic lands of Sanford Farm lend themselves easily to anyone wishing to walk a few miles on relatively level ground. To get a good dose of the spirit of this property, first explore its main trail that starts at the parking area immediately off the south side of Madaket Road. The most popular "end" to this trail is at a barn about 1.8 miles from the parking area, but the walk can be as long as you want to make it.

Walking this main trail is almost too easy to need directions. From the parking area, walk through the wooden turnstile and directly onto the main trail, taking time to check out the lily pad-choked Waqutaquaib Pond to the east below the trail. This pond drains into Head of the Hummock, a larger pond—and, at 16 feet, Nantucket's deepest—just south of the lily pads. A narrow ditch connects Head of the Hummock to the northern end of Hummock Pond, the long slender pond in the distance to the southeast.

Keeping the ponds on your left, follow the main trail—called Ram Pasture Road on the Foundation's map of Nantucket—through the open fields and into a thicket of wetland vegetation. On your first visit, be careful not to be tempted down any of the trails branching off into the brush, but once you've walked Sanford Farm a few times, the Foundation's map will make it easier for you to explore the property on your own.

To follow the main trail, remain on Ram Pasture Road as it passes a turn toward a grove of pitch pine trees. Introduced to Nantucket by Josias Folger in 1942, pitch pines prosper on Nantucket because of their resistance to salt spray and resilience in sandy soils.

Moving away from the pitch pine grove, the main trail weaves through a thicket and exits into another meadow. Ignore the trail coming in from behind on the left—this is part of a series of loops that are explained later. As Ram Pasture Road reenters the thicket at the southern end of this meadow, you'll find that it gradually begins to climb and, after a slow turn westward and then a sharp curve to the southeast, eventually opens up onto a knoll where the barn is located.

Ram Pasture and the Ocean

Length: 6.3 miles
Difficulty Rating: ***
Dogs: Yes
Children: Yes

The lure of the ocean and nearby Hummock Pond can be so strong that some walkers ignore the main walk through Sanford Farm and power-walk right out past the barn, down to Ram Pasture, and on to the ocean in about 30 to 45 minutes. If this sounds appealing, it is easily done. Once at the barn, continue on the main trail, which leads to Ram Pasture, the large field between the barn and the ocean.

When presented with a fork in the road, go right. Follow this road as it arcs roughly westward. The tall grass of the pasture will be on your left. After about 100 yards or so, take the next left to the south toward the ocean. The trail meanders down along Clark Cove on your right and then curves southeast toward a fence between pasture and dunes. At this point, look for an opening in the fence. To explore the beach, go through this opening and follow the trail through the dunes to the beach.

Back in the pasture, the trail runs east along the fence. You'll find another opening near the ocean end of Hummock Pond useful for explorations of the narrow barrier beach that keeps the ocean from washing into Hummock Pond. From this second opening, the trail skirts the edge of Hummock Pond, heading northeast, and eventually rejoins the main trail leading back to the barn and eventually the parking area on Madaket Road.

Pond Explorations

The Sanford Farm property is bordered on three sides by water: Hummock Pond to the east, Clark Cove to the southwest, and the Atlantic Ocean to the southeast. Luckily, there are several good trails leading to the edge of each body of water.

While you're walking the main trails on this land, you'll encounter other mown trails that branch off into the thicket, tempting you to explore them. Do so with vigor, for they lead to meadows and shoreline areas replete with aquatic wildlife at certain times of the year. Loops and excursions off the main path present themselves almost immediately after you leave the parking area up on Madaket Road.

Head of the Hummock

Good views of Head of the Hummock, along with the ditch connecting it to Hummock Pond, can found along this first loop. After descending into the meadow from the parking area, just past the ruins of an old farm on your right, to the northwest, walk left toward the grove of pitch pine trees. Beyond the grove, this loop leads toward the pond, rising up with good views to the east, then drops down toward the rushes lining the pond and meanders southwest back to reconnect with the main trail. After you have walked through a sand pit-like section of the trail and the trail has turned sharply to the southwest, keep your eyes open for a left turn onto a trail that dead-ends right at the shore of the pond.

This loop adds about two tenths of a mile to a walk straight out to the barn and back on Ram Pasture Road.

Clark Cove

If you choose to walk the loop around Ram Pasture after soaking up the amazing view at the barn, there's a great way to see the inland shore of Clark Cove just before you reach the beach. Follow the directions above in the "Ram Pasture and the Ocean" loop to get to Clark Cove. After you take the left that leads to Clark Cove and the beach, be on the lookout for a right turn to the west.

This mown path will take you closer to the pond. Follow it west toward the pond and then northeast along its western shore. Walk along the pond and note how the rushes and cattails gradually tighten the pond to a narrow strip of water.

Near the end of the pond, the trail turns sharply right to the south. Remain on this trail and you'll end up back at the turn for the trail that leads down to the beach. This pond loop will add about 1.2 miles to your walk out to the beach.

Hummock Pond

Short of paddling a kayak or canoe on Hummock Pond, the best way to take a good long look at this salt pond is to walk a short loop off the eastern side of the Ram Pasture loop trail. If you walk around Ram Pasture by going to Clark Cove first, you won't reach the eastward turn for this loop near Hummock Pond until you've nearly circled the pasture. So, instead of going right toward Clark Cove at the fork leading into Ram Pasture from the barn trail, go left and look for a left, the trail that runs northeast down to a meadow in the direction of the pond. Walk north-northeast through this meadow and you'll discover great views of the pond and its shoreline.

Avoid following a trail that appears to trace the shoreline. Even in the driest of island weather, the land surrounding Nantucket's ponds is soggy, and in many cases, you'll find unforgiving mud that's no fun to tramp through. Instead, in the left corner of the meadow, follow the trail that returns you to the main path, headed toward the barn, and add only half a mile to your walk.

Clark Cove to Ram Pasture

Length: 6.2 Miles
Difficulty Rating: ****
Dogs: Yes (leashed)
Children: Yes

For many walkers on Nantucket, the destination is always the beach, no matter what the time of year. Since almost all of the paths in the Sanford Farm property end up at the beach, beach and shore lovers will be happy walking anywhere on these lands. This loop includes a stretch of this property and is, for the most part, off the well-trod paths of Sanford Farm.

Because this is one of the longer walks in this book, bring plenty of water, fruit, energy bars and other trail food, and allow about three to four hours for the walk. It can be done in two and a half hours, but that's without stopping for more than a few minutes. Needless to say, a good pair of walking shoes is essential for total enjoyment. Your dogs will love this one, but small children may find it grueling. From the Sanford Farm parking lot, walk back out the driveway and turn left (west) onto the bike path that ultimately ends at Madaket Beach. To the south of the path, just after leaving the parking area, the bike path affords a great view of the Sanford Farm property.

In this area, the Nantucket Land Bank cleared invasive scrub oak and re-established native grass fields. In March or April, this is a prime area to observe the phenomenal dusk and dawn courtship flight and song of the male woodcock. You'll hear his steady call, *peent-peent-peent*, before he flies skyward out of sight then rapidly spirals down, with his wings making a distinctive whistling sound, to land within feet and sometimes inches of where he left the ground.

After enjoying the view and searching for the woodcock, walk along the bike path. Shortly after passing a green picnic table, take a left down a dirt road called Barrett Farm Road, the first left after the second parking area for this property. If you must avoid the bike path at the start of this walk, you can park in this small parking area, owned by the Land Bank, at the start of Barrett Farm Road. This road will take you all the way to Clark Cove and the ocean.

Once on Barrett Farm Road, take the left at the first fork. After about a half-mile of navigating mud puddles and catching odd glimpses of the ocean to the south and of the Madaket Landfill to the west, you'll come to a 90-degree left turn. This turn will lead you right into the Sanford Farm property, but to continue on the full walk, avoid this turn and keep side-stepping the puddles and walking toward the sound of the ocean roaring in the distance. Once beyond the worst of the puddles, you'll pass through a stand of pine trees and, about 100 feet later, encounter a fork in the road. Go left and keep your eyes open for the inland parts of Clark Cove.

Eventually, you'll arrive at another fork that merely offers a detour to the pond. Take this turn, roughly southeast toward the pond, if you want to get a good look at Clark Cove and the waterfowl that flock to this relatively new pond because of its remote location away from most of the island's human and dog population. This small spur quickly rejoins the dirt road that traces the pond out to its beach end.

From the beach, walk inland along the edge of the ocean end of Clark Cove, approaching a dune, and find the trail that leads northeast into the beach grass and toward Ram Pasture. Upon reaching a fence, step through a gap in the fence, over the wooden step, and head up-country, keeping the pond on your left. You're now in Ram Pasture and about four miles from the parking area.

There is much to see along the way back to the starting point. Walking along this side of the pond places you a lot closer to the pole that usually hosts an active osprey nest from spring through summer. See if you can count how many chicks are in it, then look east of the low shrubs of Ram Pasture and see if you can spot a northern harrier swooping low and hovering in the wind in search of furry, four-legged lunchmeat. Sometimes in the early morning and at dusk you'll see deer bounding across the pasture and through the brush. And in spring, the never-silent red-winged black birds are perched on the cattails, loudly marking their soggy territory.

It's easy to see why some people will devote a half-day to this walk. As you walk away from the pond, you'll eventually come to a T-intersection. Turn right, and you can follow this main trail all the way back upland to the Sanford Farm parking lot, or, to avoid the more populous route, turn left and follow the trail as it runs along a long, wide, straight section of grassy trail—a favorite nibbling ground for rabbits. At the end of this stretch of trail is a large, brown steel gate. Walk around it and follow the trail north and then left (west), ignoring all turns.

This dirt road will take you back to Barrett Farm Road. At the intersection, turn right and follow Barrett Farm Road out to the Madaket Road bike path that will lead you back to the parking lot.

Loop into Ram Pasture

Length: 5.2 Miles
Difficulty Rating: ***
Dogs: Yes (leashed)
Children: Yes

If you'd prefer a shorter walk, use the directions to find Barrett Farm Road off Madaket Road. Follow Barrett Farm Road, go left at the first fork, and then take the next proper left turn and follow this road, taking care to go right at the first intersection you come to. Then follow the road past the giant brown metal gate and down a long straightaway, ignoring a marked turn down to the ocean if that's not in your plans. Stay on this trail as it passes Ram Pasture to the south, and follow it as it turns left (northward) and ascends a hill to the barn. From the barn, follow the trail north-northeast to the parking lot.

Getting There

Follow Madaket Road for about 1.5 miles from its start at Caton Circle at the top of Main Street. At the top of a hill, after passing Maxcy Pond in a hollow to the north, turn left into a parking lot enclosed on three sides by split rail fencing. NRTA riders should board the Madaket bus, either in town or out in Madaket, get off at either the Swift Rock Road or Eel Point Road stop, and walk north-northeast. Walkers and cyclists can reach the start of these walks by following the Madaket bike path that originates at Caton Circle, at the intersection of Quaker Street, Upper Main Street, New Lane, and Madaket Road.

WOODCOCK

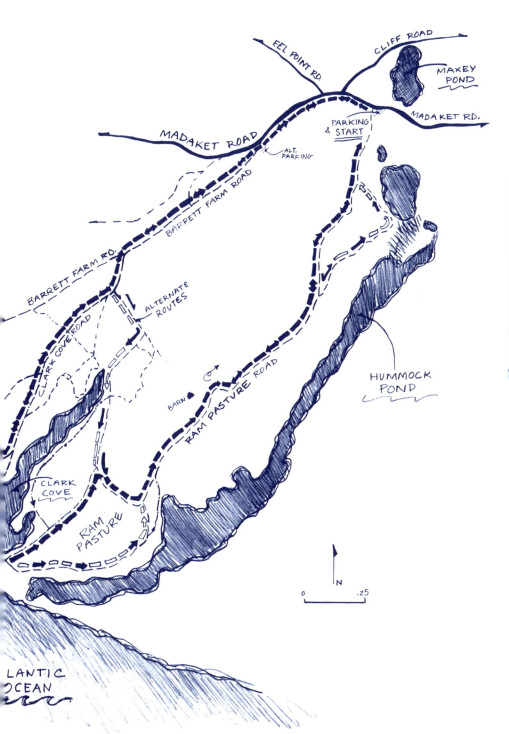

Tupancy Links

Difficulty Rating: **
Dogs: Yes
Children: Yes

.8 miles

The Area

Sallie Gail and Oswald A. "Tup" Tupancy had the spirit of Nantucket's walking public in mind when they donated the old Nantucket Golf Course to the Nantucket Conservation Foundation back in 1976. To preserve the open space oasis known as Tupancy Links, Sallie and Tup deposited the land—rolling fields on Nantucket's North Shore, just west of the wealthy populated Cliff area of the island—into the Foundation's conservation vault in perpetuity.

The original nine holes of the golf course were landscaped in 1921 by the island's first foray into golf, the Nantucket Golf Course, and for the first several years, the grass was kept shorn almost down to the nubs by 200 sheep and 50 angora goats. But Tup wasn't the first Nantucketer to let sheep loose on his land. Nantucket's 27 or so original settlers were sheep farmers before fishing, whaling, and tourism ever entered the island's employment lexicon. At one time, tens of thousands of sheep roamed the entire island, then nothing more than open fields with small pockets of forested land.

At the fledgling links, a large tent served as the clubhouse until 1926, when a permanent structure was built and nine more holes were added. In 1949, Tup, who'd come to Nantucket to be the golf pro at the Sankaty Head Golf Club, bought nine of the eighteen holes from the Nantucket Golf Course. He ran the course for four years before closing it for good.

This property has a perfect history of passive, non-destructive use and human respect for its fields, low brush, Japanese black and pitch pines, shad bush, and its coastal bluff.

What You'll See

Take a look around as you walk out over the fairways and rolling greens long since gone to seed, and you'll see development slowly creeping up on all sides. Nantucket is lucky that Tup had such incredible foresight—and Nantucket's walkers are lucky that this walk offers such easy rewards.

Tupancy Links and its bluff, which overlooks Nantucket Sound, are ideal spots to watch sunsets, sunrises, and moonrises, because you can see so much of the island and Nantucket Sound while the colors change with fading or increasing light. Great Point is 7.8 miles to the east, Coatue cuts a sandy ribbon from Great Point back to town between Nantucket Harbor and Nantucket Sound, sailboats play in the wind, and Tuckernuck Island lies to the west.

The bluff rises 42 feet above the beach, but resist any adventurous notions of hopping the low wire fence between you and the edge and climbing down to the beach. Not only would you be risking injury, but you would also dislodge more of the loose soil that comprises the bluff itself, which already gets plenty of erosion help from storm waves and rain runoff. In other words, here's where you hearken back to Tup's respect for his land and try to do the same with the acres he left for you to enjoy. The Foundation estimates the long-term erosion rate for this bluff at 3.8 feet a year. Please don't do anything to increase this number.

If it's windy, Tupancy Links is an ideal place to fly a kite—even if you're a graduate of the Charlie Brown School of Kite-Flying, because there are no trees within kite-eating distance. However, heed my warnings about ticks and poison ivy.

When to Go

Go out to this spot on a clear night to check out the stars. Try it on a not-too-cold January evening, or when the autumn leaves are in full color. Pick whichever season suits you, and don't forget essential walking companions like your children or your dogs.

The Walk

This property is accessed from the Foundation parking area off Cliff Road, where you have two choices for starting your walk. Go through the wooden turnstile at the north side of the parking lot and then take whichever path you like.

Most walkers seem to prefer going straight up the small rise and then angling right down across the field and up to the bluff, but if you veer left, taking the wood chip path through the pine grove just west of the fork in the trail, you can complete the Tupancy Links walk as a loop. Once through the pine grove, find your way out onto a gravel road that will lead you over a rise and eventually down to the bluff overlooking Nantucket Sound.

Follow this road, with the split rail fence on your left, up a rise from which you can see back into town, including, to the northeast, the steeple of the First Congregational Church on Centre Street and, to the southeast, the clock tower of the Unitarian Universalist Church on Orange Street and possibly the masts of the taller sailing yachts in the harbor. Continue on to the bottom of this small hill, heading right as the trail turns to wood chips and runs up to the top of the bluff overlooking the Sound. For me, this is the best part of Tup's old golf course.

When you're ready to walk back to the parking lot, stroll back down toward the links. When the trail splits, choose the left path and follow it down into a hollow. At the low point in this depression, look back toward town to get a sense of Nantucket before development.

Return to the parking lot by walking up to the crest of the rise and following the trail back out to Cliff Road.

Getting There

By auto or by bike, travel about 1.6 miles out from town on Cliff Road. When you spot the left turn for Crooked Lane, look to the right to see the beginning of a split rail fence that edges both the bike path and the old golf course and leads up into a gravel parking lot on the north side of the road. If you're traveling from Madaket, turn left onto Cliff Road just after the intersection with Eel Point Road. Wind your way past the water tower on a hill to the northeast and past Maxcy Pond to the south. On the north side of the road, just past Washing Pond Road to the north and Wannacomet Road to south, is the Tupancy Links parking area. NRTA bus riders should take the Madaket bus, get off at the Crooked Lane stop, and walk roughly northwest, following the split rail fence to the parking lot.

PITCH PINE

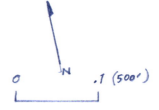

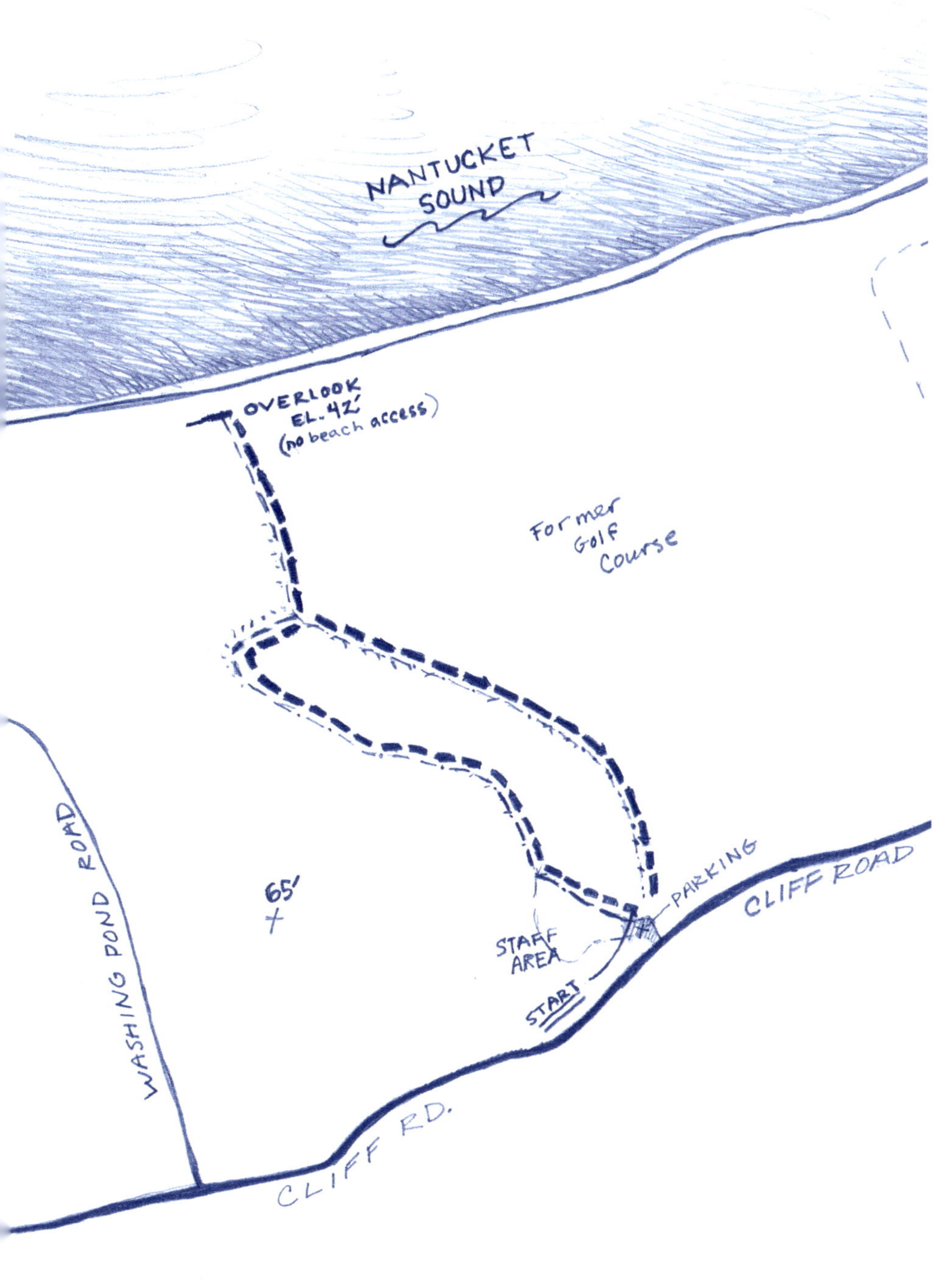

NANTUCKET SOUND

OVERLOOK EL. 42'
(no beach access)

Former Golf Course

65'
+

WASHING POND ROAD

PARKING

CLIFF ROAD

STAFF AREA

START

CLIFF RD.

129 • WALKING NANTUCKET • TUPANCY LINKS

Forests

It was not called the Old Forest without reason, for it was indeed, ancient, a survivor of vast forgotten woods; and in it there lived yet, ageing no quicker than the hills, the fathers of the fathers of the trees, remembering times when they were lords.

— J.R.R. Tolkien, The Fellowship of the Ring

133 + **Lost Farm Sanctuary**

141 + **Masquetuck**

147 + **Quidnet Route from Polpis Road**

Lost Farm Sanctuary

.8 miles

Difficulty Rating: **
Dogs: Yes
Children: Yes

The Area

Where can you sit and watch mute swans turn their tail feathers skyward to plunge their beaks into the murky shallows of pond water in search of a bottom scum salad? Hummock Pond; where you're almost always downwind and out of earshot of these magnificent birds. Sure, you can drive to First Bridge on Madaket Road and try to glimpse these swans way off at the north end of Long Pond, but the swans seem to know the secluded places that land creatures can't reach without a good pair of binoculars or a boat. The twisted and cove-lined shore of Long Pond is one of those hideouts. Fortunately for anyone hoping to see the mute swans up close, Hummock Pond is not quite the refuge from humans that the birds may think it is. A skinny, southwest-arcing trench of reed-lined water—the Hummock, as some Nantucketers call it—is a haven for all waterfowl, salt and freshwater. For this reason, the Lost Farm is a designated sanctuary of the Massachusetts Audubon Society.

But the sanctuary isn't entirely pond and shoreline, it's upland meadows, pine groves, and swamps—all open for your explorative adventures.

What You'll See

Before you reach the pond and while walking through the meadow leading down to the water, watch for red-tail and Cooper's hawks, northern harriers, and from dusk into the evening, barn owls. From spring through fall at water's edge, you can observe kingfishers, blue and white fishing birds that inhabit the shores of ponds and rivers plunging into the water for small fish. Soaring high above the pond are osprey, also called fishhawks, which spot native fish like herring, yellow perch, and pickerel, and then plummet into the pond to grab their meal.

The swans can often be found at the tip of John's Point, a peninsula of cattails on the east side of Hummock Pond. Because this land mass juts to within a hundred feet or so of the western shore of Hummock Pond, the border of the Sanford Farm property owned by the Nantucket Conservation Foundation, it pinches the pond into a narrows. Wintering ducks such as mallards, buffleheads, redheads, mergansers, and wood ducks along with great blue and black-crowned night herons, gulls, cormorants, and swans seem to congregate here, where it is easier to forage for food in the shallower water and where the pond is relatively sheltered.

However, don't expect to see the swans every time you take this walk. The mute swans that inhabit Nantucket fly among Clark Cove, Long Pond, Miacomet Pond, and Hummock Pond, depending on their feeding and mating needs. This species of swan, introduced to the U.S. from Europe in the nineteenth century, is an invasive water bird with an aggressive disposition. Much like scrub oak and pitch pine that eventually dominates lesser plants on open land in the moors, the mute swan tends to drive smaller waterfowl out of its habitat. Nonetheless, they are magnificent birds.

While at the edge of the pond checking out the swans, take note of the stalks of the cattails just beneath the surface of the water and you will see ivory barnacles. Unlike the northern rock barnacles that grow on rocks and boat hulls in the ocean, these barnacles thrive in slightly salty to fresh water. Their larvae find their way into Hummock Pond because the town

opens this pond to the ocean twice a year to increase its salinity with saltwater and to let herring and eels in and out to breed. (For a detailed explanation of pond openings, read the Quidnet Route from Polpis Road walk on page 147.) According to Nantucket's Marine Department, the barnacles' existence this far into the pond is healthy proof that the biannual pond openings are good for Hummock Pond.

When to Go

Taking this walk when the wind is fairly strong and steady is a good idea for two reasons: the wonderful whispering effect of the pine grove and the distant roar of waves breaking on Cisco Beach.

This is a loop that's great to do around sunset at any time of the year. My favorite seasons for observing the swans are spring and summer, but fall and winter reveal the scores of migratory birds that use the pond for refuge and food. Another great reason for an autumn walk is the vibrant colors of poison ivy climbing up the pine trees.

The Walk

From the parking area, walk past the steel cable that blocks vehicle traffic into the property, and you'll see the start of a pine grove. Walk to the right of it and follow the dirt and grass road as it angles right, then left, into the pines. Once you're among the pines, the thick carpet of rust-colored needles and the low branches will make you feel like you're in some dense, off-island forest. Within the pine grove are clusters of hawthorn trees, most recognizable by their sturdy one-and-a-half-inch thorns.

Be careful in your navigation, because the property is crisscrossed with a maze of deer trails, and it's quite easy to become lost. Upon entering the grove, remember to keep on the trail that is close to the brush-cut field to the west. Follow that trail as it gradually arcs toward the west. This end of the property is owned by the Nantucket Island Lands Bank.

The Land Bank, in an ongoing effort to manage its holdings properly, periodically brush-cuts much of the woody vegetation to restore this property to the grasslands that existed before dominant shrubs and trees began their invasion. You'll cross part of this open brush-cut area and re-enter the pine grove, where shortly you'll encounter a fork in the trail usually marked by a Massachusetts Audubon sign. Go right, then take the next right as it splits decisively away from the main trail and down into a clearing. Stay on this well-worn trail as it turns to the left and then ascends a short rise.

Once you top the rise, a long meadow spreads out before you. From this vantage, you should be able to catch glimpses of the pond and Sanford Farm rising out of the reeds on the pond's western shore. Walk down into the meadow, taking care to keep to the right without wandering off into the swamp. This path will ultimately lead you to the edge of the pond.

Walk south along the water, following a trail that traces the shore and occasionally swerves inland toward the pines. After the second of these deviations dips you down into a dell and then up a small rise, walk toward the water again on the shore trail to find the peninsula described above.

After enjoying the swans, return to the woods by walking back to the shore trail and continuing south into a small clearing. From this grassy area, you should see the back of another Massachusetts Audubon sign fronting two wooden posts to the left. Pass the sign and follow the trail as it opens up into the long meadow that led you to the pond. Now walk away from the pines and out onto the meadow, roughly northeast toward the swamp north of the meadow path, until you find the trail on which you originally entered the meadow. Follow this trail back to the parking area. If you don't want to return to Millbrook Road right away, you can explore a trail that continues south of the Audubon sign and the clearing through the pines, and past the sanctuary plant ecologist's residence, and out into more Land Bank land.

A steady pace around this loop takes about 45 minutes. Once you get your bearings and know how to find your way back to Millbrook Road, you can

spend a couple of hours following each little trail you discover and really getting the run of the property.

If you're interested in other Massachusetts Audubon sanctuaries and want to learn more about this conservation organization, log onto their Web site at *http://www.massaudubon.org/*.

Getting There

This walk is accessible from Millbrook Road off the south side of Madaket Road. About a mile west of Caton Circle, at the bottom of a dip in Madaket Road just after Maxcy Pond Road to the north (right), you will see Millbrook on the left. If traveling by NRTA, take the Madaket route and get off at the Millbrook Road stop.

Walk, drive, or pedal southwest down Millbrook and just before the asphalt ends at a gravel driveway marked by a concrete public way post, hook a hard left and continue down the pavement that quickly turns to dirt. Stay on this sandy track for about 200 yards until you see, on your left (to the south), a grassy parking area surrounded by a split-rail fence. Park and enter the sanctuary, walking southwest past a steel cable coated with orange plastic.

.8 miles

Difficulty Rating: *
Dogs: No
Children: Older children

The Area

The Wampanoag name for Quaise is Masquetuck. My word for Masquetuck is "otherworldly." Those familiar with J.R.R. Tolkien's *The Hobbit* and the *Lord of the Rings* trilogy can draw on a Middle-Earth frame of reference and let the 13.5-acre Masquetuck Reservation absorb them into its enchanted forest at the edge of the marsh surrounding the west lobe of Polpis Harbor. They may see this part of Nantucket through a Hobbit's eyes.

A tranquil spot, Masquetuck is a shining example of the conservation effort on Nantucket. In 1990, the Nantucket Conservation Foundation purchased part of this property from Robert and Cynthia Jay, who donated the rest to the Foundation.

Its beauty and ecological diversity are immediately captivating. Sensitive and fragile soils are held in place by partially exposed root systems that, if damaged, could spell death for the trees. When you take this walk, remember the reverence Bilbo and Frodo had for their mystical environment and imagine what the island would be like without special spots like Masquetuck.

Masquetuck is not really a walk for distance. Instead, it is a tour through Nantucket's diverse ecosystems: it is an ideal place to experience several varied habitats in a relatively small area. In about 20 minutes, you can walk through upland field, forest, swamp, and saltmarsh, and there are plenty of plant and animal species for you catalogers out there.

What You'll See

As you enter the trail, notice some fine distinctions among the large trees. White oak leaves have round lobes, and their bark has broad, scaly, loose ridges. Black oak leaves have pointed lobes, often with bristly tips, and the bark has elongated fissures. The oaks prefer the drier soil conditions, while the red maples, the large trees in the low wet spots, have shallow, spreading root systems that enable them to get sufficient oxygen near the soil surface. As you walk through this woodland, richly layered in mosses, lichens, ferns, shrubs, and trees, listen for woodpeckers and other bird sounds. Feel the softness of the trail padded with leaf litter, unlike most of the other walks you may have taken on Nantucket, and watch the light filter through the high treetop canopy.

The island's founding residents quickly used the limited stock of large trees on the island to build houses and boats, to heat homes, and to grow crops. The newly cleared land was then kept treeless by grazing sheep, thus large trees on Nantucket today are a rarity and definitely provoke a feeling of excitement for those of us who live on the island year-round.

In the moist, boggy areas in the forest at the start of this walk are sphagnum moss, skunk cabbage, and waist-high ferns growing under black tupelo and swamp maples. Near the end of this trail, fat, squat scrub oaks line the trail out to the saltmarsh cordgrass and mud.

If you can, log onto the Conservation Foundation's Web site (see Appendix) for a good explanation of what you've seen at Masquetuck.

When to Go

When I go out to Masquetuck, it's usually in fall, winter and early spring, when the bugs aren't around. There are lots of breeding spots in this moist, shaded area for mosquitoes that like to nibble on bare legs and arms. Enjoy Masquetuck in the colder months and take your time examining some of Nantucket's largest and oldest trees.

In spring, at dusk, listen for peepers and the crook-crook of black-crowned night herons. During the day, red-winged blackbirds guard nests in the swamp, catbirds call incessantly, and the occasional osprey can be seen hovering over Polpis Harbor looking for fish.

The Walk

Just beyond the cul-de-sac on Quaise Pasture Road and over the split rail fence, you can walk into a small field and down to the marsh for a glimpse of Polpis Harbor and Pocomo beyond before entering the forest on the trail next to the large white oak. Follow the trail through the tall trees across the leaf-strewn ground that is almost always soggy.

My favorite part of the walk leads out onto a small point on the Polpis Harbor shore past an old white oak with multiple trunks growing out of its base. To see these wonderful oaks, take a left where the trail splits after it crosses a pair of wooden planks over a small muddy drainage ditch. A narrow path loops around this point, which juts out into the harbor.

Taking a right at the fork will lead you up into a small beech grove. Here, moss covers the exposed roots of the trees, and both of these swamp plants are extremely sensitive to foot traffic. Try to avoid stepping on the roots and scraping off the moss. Also, the low beeches may be inviting to tree climbers young and old, but I don't recommend attempting these trees. Falling will result in scrapes, cuts, and possibly broken limbs—both yours and the trees'.

Beyond the enormous beech tree out along the shoreline, I sometimes see a lone great blue heron wading through the shallows, spearing fish with its knife-like bill.

Don't forget to include your children on this walk, because this is a perfect introduction to the island's natural world. But leave your dogs at home because they're bound to dig up and destroy delicate soils and plants.

Getting There

Quaise Pasture Road is on the north side of Polpis Road, which has its own bike path. On the NRTA's 'Sconset via Polpis Road route, the bus stops at Quaise Road. About 100 yards east along Polpis Road, look for Quaise Pasture Road on the left. Follow this road as it turns from asphalt to gravel and ends in a circle with maroon Nantucket Conservation Foundation markers near an opening in a split rail fence. These mark the entrance to the property

OAK LEAVES

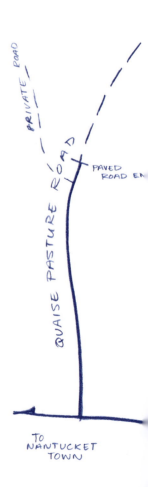

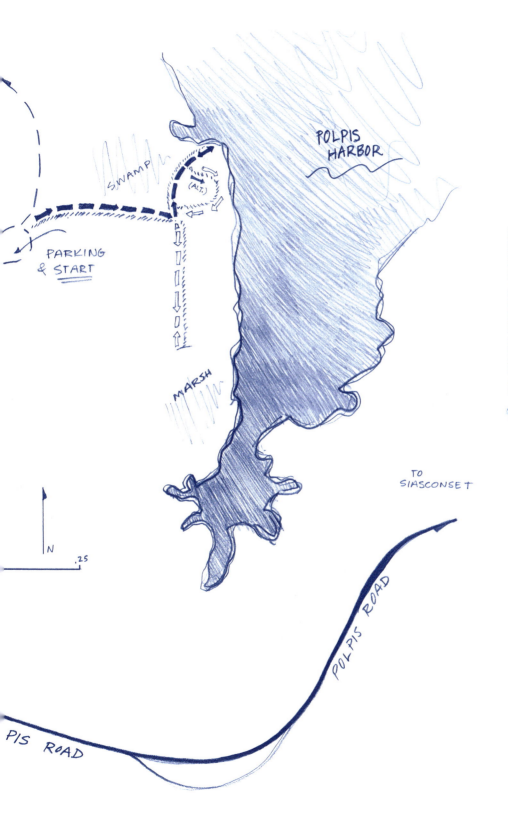

Quidnet Route from Polpis Road

.9 miles

Difficulty Rating: *
Dogs: Yes
Children: Yes

The Area

When you pass by Sesachacha Pond on Polpis Road, views of this great salt pond on the edge of Quidnet village are brief at best. You can see more of the pond as you pedal by on the bike path, but Sesachacha is much more enjoyable when you walk around it.

It's easy to miss the narrow dirt road that leads to Sesachacha Pond in its northwestern corner, as well as a place to park for this walk. The access road affords fishers and bird watchers the chance to walk partially around the pond, but just how much of Sesachacha's shores you can explore depends solely on its water level. Since 1993, the town has been opening this pond to the ocean in spring and fall. Along with bleeding the pond of excess water, laying bare its shores, the openings allow American eels and blueback herring to change ecosystems for six months at a time.

The blueback herring and American eels are two fish species that need both salt water and freshwater environments to thrive. The American eel, called a catadromous fish because it breeds in salt water and lives a majority of its life in fresh to brackish water, swims out of the pond to spawn in the sea in the spring, and young eels swim into Sesachacha during the fall opening. Conversely, the blueback herring is an anadromous fish because it spawns in the relatively fresh waters of Sesachacha Pond, swimming in to the pond during the spring opening and out to the ocean at the fall opening. About half of the pond itself and the land surrounding it—88 acres—are owned by the Massachusetts

Audubon Society, which welcomes the public to visit the property. The Society's Sesachacha heathlands sanctuary is one of 37 wildlife sanctuaries in the state, and one of 18 unstaffed.

What You'll See

As a sanctuary, the Sesachacha heathlands are practically free of the vestiges of civilization. Poke around these shores starting at the little parking area off Polpis Road, and you can spot—depending on the season—ocean birds, such as eider ducks, long-tailed ducks, gulls, and cormorants, that spend the winter on Nantucket and use both the pond and small marsh near the road as shelter. You'll be tempted to spend all your time near the pond and along its shores, but proceed with this walk for about 20 minutes, and you'll discover a beautiful view of the pond and the rest of the Massachusetts Audubon Society's Sesachacha property, which lies inland from the pond.

You'll see little deer trails running all over the meadow below the small hill on this walk. If you're lucky enough to be downwind when up on the rise, you might see some deer pass by. Watch the sky long enough, and you'll see red-tailed hawks and northern harriers scanning the brush for rodents. With binoculars, you can see ospreys, great blue herons, and great egrets looking for fish and frogs down near the pond.

When to Go

When the island's population explodes in the summer, this walk is an escape to a quiet, secluded place. In spring, you can watch the island wake up from winter, and in fall, you will see foliage more common in Vermont, Maine, and New Hampshire. Winter means occasional snow in the forests and, if the weather cooperates, ice on the pond—a rare treat on Nantucket.

The Walk

Ironically, this secluded trail is almost too easily found for this to be a private spot. After leaving the parking area on the southwestern edge of the pond, walk northwest away from 'Sconset on Polpis Road. Count the telephone poles from the pond access; between the second and third, you'll find the remainder of an asphalt apron leading down into what used to be a dirt road on the east side of the road. Turn right down this trail and follow it as it snakes left and right, heading generally north-northeast. After several hundred yards, you'll pass one of the thickest, gnarliest bramble patches you'll ever encounter. It's difficult to imagine how even a small rabbit or spotted turtle could make it through the dense snarl of thorns and remain unscratched.

The maze of wooded swamps and kettle ponds in the northwestern section of the island is primary habitat to a sizable population of spotted turtles, a Species of Special Concern in the state of Massachusetts. Within the dark water, muck, and leaf litter in these areas, the turtles find camouflage in the yellow spots on their dark shells.

The trail will straighten out past the bramble, and on the right, you'll see the wavy trunks of black tupelo trees twisting toward the sky. As the trail takes a turn to the right, you'll see on the left what appears to be the beginning of a road. About 100 feet from that point, take a right into the stand of black tupelo. Follow this trail toward the swamp to the east, then to the right along the swamp and back in the direction you came.

Be alert to a variety of birdcalls, and keep your eyes peeled for salamanders and spotted, painted, and snapping turtles. This trail is a tricky one, so refer to the map if you feel you're getting lost. The trail skirts the swamp, heading up to the left (east) and eventually opening into a small glade. Continue east through this glade, following the trail as it arcs right to the south and then opens up into a meadow facing Sesachacha Pond.

From there, walk generally west and then up a small rise to the right (southwest) and plant yourself in the grass. From this spot, you can see Sesachacha end to end, the red stripe of Sankaty Lighthouse in the distance across the pond, and east out to the ocean beyond. In fall, the views of the moors to the west are spectacular.

When ready to leave, return the way you came in, out through the small glade, along the swamp, and back to the trail. Once at the trail, turn left and follow it back to Polpis Road. But be careful. There are miles and miles of faint deer paths that may appear at first to be human trails but usually disappear into the bush where only the deer can go. Attempts to explore these trails will spoil wilderness that is the terrain of island animals, and repeated incursions into these areas may eventually wear out our welcome on Mass Audubon properties on Nantucket.

Getting There

From the Rotary at the end of Orange Street, follow Milestone Road to Polpis Road and travel about six miles, watching for the dirt road leading to the pond. If you're coming from Siasconset, travel 2.8 miles, passing a small turnout overlooking the pond, and turn right to the parking area immediately after the pond. From town, NRTA bus riders should take the 'Sconset via Polpis route and get off at the 334 Polpis Road stop; from Siasconset, take the same bus and get off at the Sankaty Head Golf Club stop.

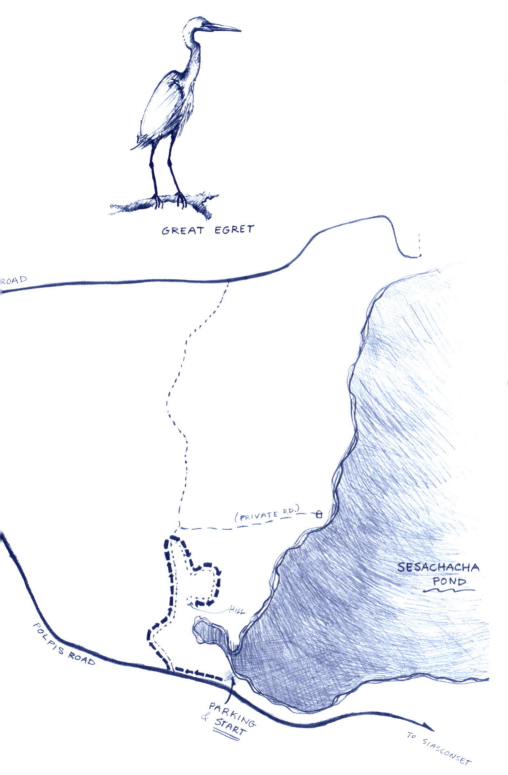

Swamps, Bogs and Ponds

> Goodbye. I am going to the banks of the great gray-green, greasy Limpopo River, all set about with fever trees, to find out what the crocodile has for dinner.
> — Rudyard Kipling, "The Elephant's Child," Just So Stories

155 + **Squam Farm**

163 + **Squam Swamp**

169 + **Tom Nevers Pond**

175 + **Windswept Cranberry Bog**

.8 miles

Difficulty Rating: **
Dogs: Yes
Children: Yes

The Area

The spotted turtle's Nantucket kingdom lies in the swamps of Squam and Quidnet. However, upon entering this perpetually wet environment, you'll soon notice that you're much more likely to see the spotted turtle's habitat than the elusive turtle itself.

In Massachusetts, the spotted turtle is a Species of Special Concern, meaning there are very few reproducing populations in the state. The wooded swamps and bogs of Nantucket appear to host some of the state's most viable populations. The Nantucket Conservation Foundation wants everyone to enjoy their Squam property (on foot), including the spotted turtles.

This rare and diminutive turtle lives on about 150 acres of land owned by the Foundation in Quidnet. This tract of shrub swamps, meadows, and hardwood forests was opened to the public for passive use in 1998. A study in several different island ecosystems for anyone interested in botany, birds, or land recovery, this walk is a great way to see the ocean from a hillock, and it's an easy hike in autumn to see the fall foliage.

What You'll See

Wildlife driven from its natural habitats elsewhere on Nantucket by development seems to have taken refuge in this part of the island. One early spring morning, I spotted four separate groups of deer, a northern harrier, several red-tail hawks, countless catbirds, towees, crows, rabbits, and one garter snake. The spring peepers can be deafening at daybreak and dusk. In the summer, the gulping, jug-a-rum chorus of green bullfrogs plays throughout the day. Also, do be on the lookout for the spotted turtle. About four inches in length, its shell is shiny black dotted with yellow spots about an inch apart.

At water level in the swamps, sphagnum moss, with its mats of greenish yellow and red stalks and its star-like branches, can be seen from several sections of the trail on this walk. Mosses don't have a developed root system or leaves. Rather, they absorb water directly into their cells by growing in moist areas close to the ground. Amazingly, sphagnum moss can hold up to twenty-five times its weight in water. This moss forms the basis of the swamp. One layer of sphagnum grows on top of another, then another and another, each bottom layer becoming more and more compressed and eventually forming into a layer of peat. You may not see water on the surface of the swamp in the middle of the summer, but if your foot were to slip into the moss, it would sink many feet down into the oozing, mucky peat.

When to Go

Don't limit yourself to the warmer seasons for exploring this property. Exploring Nantucket during winter is a must for anyone who loves this island. The sky, the air, the, ocean, the landscape—all of it is different in winter. And don't forget the swamps. With the leaves off the trees and bushes, you'll get a better, longer look into what is most often shrouded in leaves and vines. Try to go right after a new snow.

Do bring your dog on a leash, but don't venture into the swamps or anywhere that is not a well-defined path. If you encounter a spotted turtle during your explorations, watch it, but don't bother it.

The Walk

From the parking area, walk northeast down the road into the woods just beyond. What remains of a jeep trail runs through the property with smaller spurs branching off along the way. This mile and a half walk usually takes about 45 minutes roundtrip, but on occasion I've spent a couple hours exploring each trail and watching the wildlife. The following directions include a number of brief, loop detours to points of interest and back to the main trail.

About 100 yards from the start of the trail, you'll encounter a meadow that opens up to the right. The trail winds through the meadow, up a small hill, and then to the southeast to a dead end at private land marked by a fence across the path.

In the meadow, thistle grows in small bunches among ground-crawling wild grapevines, and sometimes you can spot hummingbirds flitting around, jabbing their needle-like beaks into the purple flowers of the thistles.

Back on the main trail, a short distance from the principal meadow, a left turn down a mown trail will lead to a simple out-and-back path. Continue on the main dirt path as it curves slowly to the right, then left, and out onto a gentle rise overlooking a small pond that dries up considerably in the summer. Right before this rise, the path forks to the right onto a grass path. Follow the grass path to the right for a short loop around the pond.

Having rounded the pond and rejoined the main trail follow its arc to the right and uphill. A large, long meadow opens up to the left of the path. Small pockets of wet meadow function as temporary ponds during periods of wet weather. An abundance of aquatic insects and green frogs procreate in these ponds and serve as a food source for turtles, particularly during spring, their most active season.

The hilltop of this meadow was part of a system of sand pits before the Land Council bought the land and regraded the pits back to meadow. The views from this hilltop are particularly enjoyable during the fall, best enjoyed with the roar of the distant Atlantic Ocean to the east, on the shores of Squam and Quidnet.

Take your time exploring this meadow and its wetlands. To return to the main trail, either go back out the way you came, or from the hilltop find a narrow path leading into the trees to the south. Once in the wooded area, the path will drop quickly into the swamp and head back toward the loop around the pond you passed earlier. As you enter the wooded area, notice on the right the small grove of beech trees, with their smooth, light gray bark and dark green, slightly toothed leaves that feel like paper.

As you stand where the water cuts through the path, notice the green sphagnum moss to your right. In the water, a clump of tussock sedge is conveniently located for placing your foot as you jump across the stream. Continue on the swamp trail to a fork. Both trail choices will deposit you out on the main trail, at which point you can either walk back to the start of this walk or do some more exploring. To continue on, walk past the turn for the hilltop you just investigated and follow the trail as it draws close to the swamp while curving southeast toward Quidnet.

Just after a right bend in the trail, walk left (east) up a small rise, and you'll catch a view of the ocean overlooking Squam Road. Do not venture further—the land ahead is private (and swampy). Return to the parking area by retracing your steps along the main path.

Getting There

Turning onto Quidnet Road from Polpis Road, proceed about 150 feet and turn left onto a dirt road across from a cluster of mailboxes. Follow this unmarked road—called Salti Way—up a gradual rise, ignoring turns to the left and right. Just after the road narrows, you'll approach a fork. If you're not already on foot, stow your ride in the fenced-in grass parking area on the right. Do not go down the right fork, a private way.

In season, you can catch the NRTA bus that runs the 'Sconset via Polpis Road Route and stops at Quidnet Road.

SPOTTED
TURTLE

POLPIS RD.

POLPIS RD.

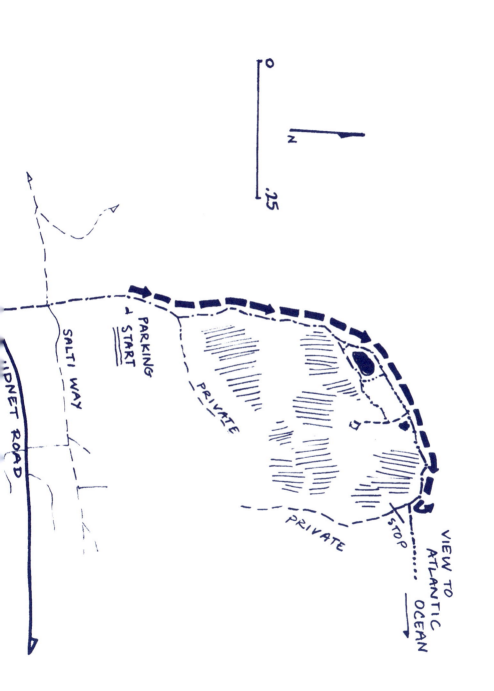

Squam Swamp

Difficulty Rating: *
Dogs: No
Children: Yes

.5 miles

The Area

Down a canopy-covered trail through the Wauwinet Road side of Squam Swamp is a 291-acre chunk of Squam Swamp owned by the Nantucket Conservation Foundation, which it purchased from Bob and Molly B. Sziklas in 1982. The Foundation, not wanting to expand the use of its prized swamp, established a nature trail through a small portion of the property to give the public a good, long look at one of the island's most prevalent wetland ecosystems: the shrub swamp.

At the start of this walk is a wooden post with a small box holding guides to the trail. This guide, combined with 19 yellow-capped, numbered posts called InfoSpots that are planted throughout the walk, make up a self-guided tour. Open up the brochure, move on to InfoSpot Number 1, and read all about what you're seeing at that part of the trail. Then follow the trail to the next InfoSpot.

As you follow the InfoSpots out into the swamp, be mindful that you're in an extremely fragile environment that could quickly deteriorate at the hands, or rather the feet, of those who don't respect the unique plants that thrive in the swamp. For this reason, please don't bring your dogs. Keep to the main trail and do not wander into the swamp. Not only will you do irreparable damage to delicate soils, grasses, scrubs, and root systems, but you can quickly become lost in this swamp.

What You'll See

In this wonderful wetland walk, deer are always just behind the next bush and just out of eyesight, bounding into the safety of the thick forest. Crows, finches, catbirds, red-tail hawks, chickadees, song sparrows, and blue jays abound. In the spring, ferns grow waist high. Serpentine black tupelo trees snake skyward, and Nantucket's version of old-growth trees Oaks, beeches, and swamp maples stand sentry on the edges of the trail. And there's even a small stream that trickles underneath the trail running south to north.

The beauty of this walk is its relative isolation from the rest of Nantucket. You know you're surrounded by water on all sides of the island, and yet this little forest seems to be completely oblivious to the finite island environment churning all around it. While you're out in the swamp, a stillness, a perfect quiet can be found here.

When to Go

I recommend avoiding the walk during spring and summer, when mosquitoes, deer flies, and other bloodsuckers are prevalent; however, bug repellent makes the Squam Swamp walk do-able in the warmer months. Autumn is the perfect time to explore this swamp, since the sparse fall foliage of Nantucket is found most abundantly in and around the island's moister ecosystems. If you're looking for finer serenity and peacefulness, try walking this trail during a snowstorm. The falling snow in the windproof forest lays a quiet over the swamp that most people never experience on Nantucket since snow is scarcer than tourists in the off-season.

The Walk

Park your car or bike in the parking area off Wauwinet Road. On the eastern side of the parking lot is a path that drops down under a thick canopy. Before starting out, take one of the map guides from the box on the post at the trailhead. Remember to return the map guide to the box when you return.

Both the guide and this book provide maps of this walk, but since the walk is marked with numbered yellow posts, it's tough to get lost. When you reach the post marked #19, you've come to the end, and you just walk back out the way you came.

I suggest experiencing this walk first by using your own senses and ignoring the InfoSpots, and then do it again, stopping to read the guide at each InfoSpot. This will give you the chance to look around with your own eyes and then to learn from the guide and the InfoSpots what you saw the first time around.

Getting There

Take Polpis Road to Wauwinet Road and travel about 1.5 miles. Roughly 100 yards after the left turn for Pocomo Road at the top of a rise, look for a right turn into a grass and dirt parking lot surrounded by a split rail fence. If traveling by bicycle, leave the Polpis Road bike path at the turn for Wauwinet Road and follow the directions above. Bus riders need to take the 'Sconset via Polpis Road bus and get off at Wauwinet Road, then travel to the parking area as above.

166 • WALKING NANTUCKET • SQUAM SWAMP

TO NANTUCKET TOWN

POLPIS ROAD

ALTAR ROCK ROAD

POLPIS HARBOR ROAD

WAUWINET ROAD

RING RD.

POLPIS ROAD

TO SIASCONSET

QUIDNET ROAD

BEECH LEAVES & NUT

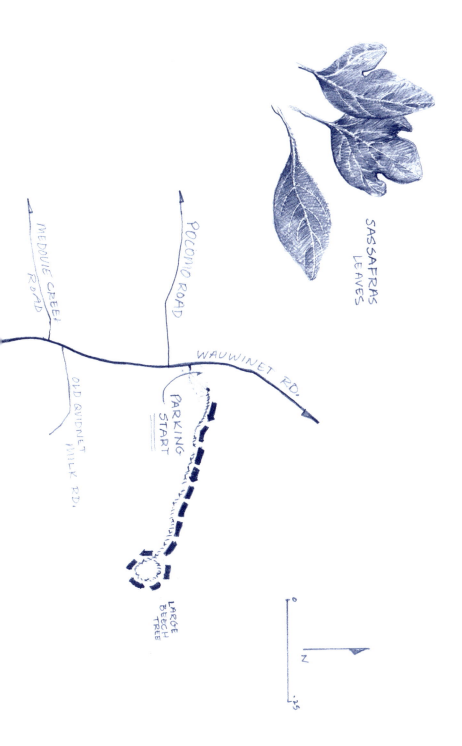

Difficulty Rating: ***
Dogs: Yes
Children: Yes

3.5 miles

The Area

Nantucket, with its rolling moors and vast expanses of beach, epitomizes the phrase "wide open spaces." But because of hollows, slight dips in the landscape, trees, rolling hills and, more recently, buildings, there are no more than a handful of spots on the island from which you can take in the scenic vistas as they were 100 years ago. The best place to see a whole lot of sky, moor, and dune—and of Massachusetts, for that matter—is at sea level at the southeastern-most point of the island, just south of the village of Siasconset.

Just off Low Beach Road in Siasconset is a U.S. Coast Guard station with a tall tower that requires a vast bare field for its support cables. On the ocean side of Low Beach Road stretches one of the island's widest dune fields, in some places separating the road from the ocean by nearly 300 yards.

These sand dunes are a natural protective shield for upland areas. The greater their width, the greater their capacity to endure the erosive power of wind and water. During winter storms, waves pound up the beach and pull sand from cliffs and dunes, carrying the sand away and redistributing it onto another beach. The wind, too, moves sand, which can help to rebuild dunes. An eastern storm can ravage southeastern dunes in the Low Beach area, while the northwestern dunes might experience less erosion. Sand taken from one dune or beach will ultimately be washed away to build up another. This dynamic is called littoral drift.

When the winter storms subside, the tides and currents are able to build up reserves in the dunes, and consequently to widen the beaches. This natural, cyclical pattern of erosion and accretion can be observed along shorelines, such as Low Beach, unencumbered by bulkheads, groins (rock jetties), or other engineered structures.

What You'll See

Standing where the asphalt part of Low Beach Road meets its dirt extension that leads to Tom Nevers Pond, you're in the middle of one of the island's largest coastal plains. You can see out over the dunes to the ocean, past the USCG tower to the moors beyond, up to Tom Nevers Head and back over to Siasconset's water tower poking up out of the trees. There's virtually nothing to block your view for several miles in all directions.

Above the pond to the southwest is Tom Nevers Head, about 65 feet in elevation, where once sat the Tom Nevers Hotel. Guests arrived from town by train, and a section of the old railroad bed, which continued on to Siasconset, is visible out in the dunes south of the pond. Tom Nevers is named for an Indian who lived nearby in the 1670s. This Native American would stand on the bluff and keep his eyes peeled for whales that washed up on the beach, ready to alert his village so the bounty from the sea could be swiftly carved up before it began to rot.

In and around the pond, you'll find gulls, several varieties of ducks, great blue herons, and even cormorants seeking a respite from the rigors of ocean life. And if you venture out to the beach in the winter, see if you can find gray and harbor seals as they sun themselves on this remote beach or play in the pounding surf. If you find yourself downwind of a sea dog on the beach, approach slowly and quietly to try for a closer look—but not close enough to touch. If a seal doesn't rush into the water when you get too close, it's either sick or resting. But this doesn't make it any less

dangerous. Do not try to touch a seal. They're quick and will bite you. The Nantucket Marine Mammal Stranding Team recommends keeping 500 feet between you and a seal.

When to Go

If you want a delightful long walk anytime of the year, follow the directions from the center of Siasconset to the end of Low Beach Road and then return the way you came. Even though there is no loop involved in this walk, it's still a beautiful hike into one of the more remote parts of Nantucket. You may also enjoy this walk at sunset or when the fog rolls in.

However, most of the route is exposed. You'll be out on what amounts to an island prairie with little protection from the wind. During the warmer months on Nantucket, the wind can be a blessing, but not during the winter. Nantucket is notorious for its howling winter winds, so dress warmly.

The Walk

Starting east of the 'Sconset Market in the center of the village, walk over the wooden footbridge that crosses Gully Road from a shell lane that starts near the market. The bridge affords you a great view of the ocean and of the sundial on the house next to the bridge. Once across the bridge, you'll be on Ocean Avenue. Walk along it, taking time to enjoy the views of the sea and the dunes. That rapids-like action you see out in the water, even on a calm day, is the Siasconset Rip, the result of two currents and the tide clashing just off the shore. Because of the rip, the fishing is great on this beach and out on the water.

Keep to this road as it gradually descends to just above sea level and becomes Low Beach Road. Low Beach Road turns to dirt just after the Coast Guard installation and a left-hand entrance to the beach. Continue walking on Low Beach Road, keeping the ocean to your left.

At the end of this dirt road, about a half mile west of the Coast Guard station and past several houses, are Tom Nevers Pond and Tom Nevers Head up beyond it. After exploring the pond area, either check out the beach or walk back to Siasconset the way you came.

Getting There

To begin this walk, park in the village of Siasconset located on Nantucket's eastern shore. To get there, travel east from the Rotary on Milestone Road or northeast on Polpis Road. Cyclists can ride either the Milestone Road or the Polpis Road bike path to reach the center of Siasconset. NRTA bus riders can choose either the 'Sconset/Town or the 'Sconset via Polpis Road route; both end up in Siasconset.

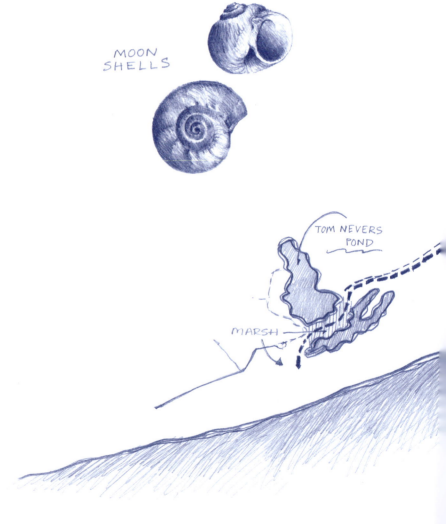

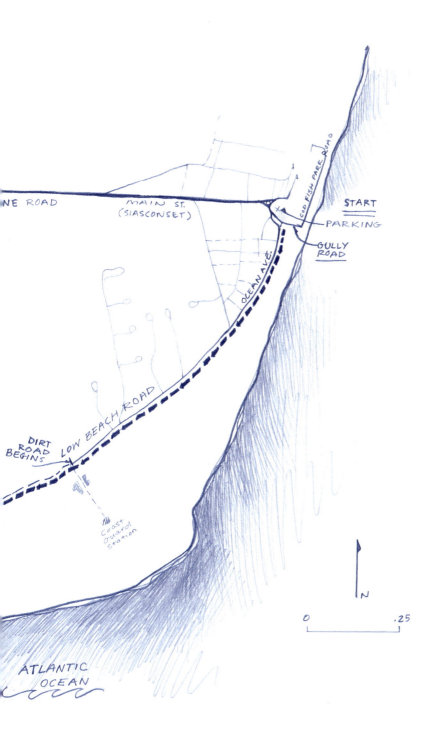

The Area

While exploring Windswept Cranberry Bog, Stump Swamp and its pond, and the trail to Almanac Pond, you'll be walking through an island wilderness area rich in diverse vegetation and wildlife. The central moors—thousands of acres of rolling hillocks covered in scrub oak, dotted with kettle hole ponds and marshes and criss-crossed by hundreds of miles of deer trails—and the cranberry bogs—are your sanctuary for two loops in this area—all preserved by the Nantucket Conservation Foundation. The bogs, including those on the north side of Milestone Road, are also under the protective wings of the NCF, and all are available for you to enjoy.

The first loop in this area is the shorter of the two and takes you around the western shore of Stump Pond rather than the eastern. As with the other loop, you'll traverse the Windswept Cranberry Bog off Polpis Road, but you'll see much more of the swamp and the pond and, with luck, see many more of the inhabitants of this wetland.

The second, longer loop, after snaking through the bogs, traces part of the eastern shore of the swamp and then breaks away into the moors. You'll walk through both thicket and wide-open space. About halfway through this loop, you'll discover a high spot for great views of the eastern end of the island.

What You'll See

Exploring these loops, you'll have the opportunity to see a curious collection of familiar animals. Ducks, great blue and black-crowned night herons, little and great egrets, and other birds thrive on the jagged, forested pond edge, on the high ground, and in the swamp. Snakes, frogs, salamanders, and turtles are also plentiful.

As you walk in spring and early summer, keep an eye out for painted, spotted, and snapping turtles dragging themselves across the trails. With both abundant food and potential mates nearby, this is their most active time of the year. But avoid making contact with any of these turtles, especially the snapping turtle. If you encounter them dragging their prehistoric-looking bodies across the dikes of the bogs or near the ponds, give these crusty old terrapins a wide berth because although they appear lethargic, they can snip off your extremities so quickly you'll scarcely feel the bite of their razor-sharp beaks.

In the skies, you'll see red-tailed hawks soaring in search of rodents, and northern harriers hovering just over the tops of the scrub oak as they scout for rabbits and smaller rodents. Out in the moors and at the forested edges of the bogs, you may see whitetail deer watching you or bounding away into the brush.

From inside the brush, you're bound to hear the song of the rufous-sided towee. One of the photographers for this book, Rob, believes there's a bird whose time on the island coincides with the seasonal visit of striped bass. When the bird arrives, his premise goes, so do the stripers … followed shortly thereafter by his own frustrating yet uncanny ability to haul in only schoolies. When the bird wings out to British Columbia for the winter, the bass disappear, according to Rob's theory.

The fabled harbinger of stripers seems to be the rufous-sided towee—*Pipilo erythrophthalmus*—a robin-sized migratory bird that thrives in Nantucket's moors. It sings two distinctive, separate songs that sound like *drink your teeeeeeee* and a short *che-wink*. Mixed in with the towee's calls, you'll hear catbird meows, red-winged blackbird noises, and a myriad of other upland and wetland bird chatter.

During early September, look for ripening wild grapes dangling from their vines. You will smell and find the grapes, growing on vines that drape themselves over trees and bushes in a suffocating net. And depending on which—if any—grower is operating the cranberry bogs, you may witness cranberries being harvested from flooded bogs.

Along the swamp trail that envelops you in branches, with the edge of the swamp drawing you closer to its water, be on the lookout for the high-bush blueberry and stands of the twisty trunks of tupelo and sassafras, shrubs and trees that love to sink their roots into moist soil. One-, two-, and three-lobed leaves distinguish the sassafras tree from the tupelo's teardrop, elliptical leaves. To prove yourself right, scrape the bark of a young sassafras twig to whiff that familiar root beer smell. The sassafrass trees also have a short-thorned, bright green vine, called catbrier, snaking up their trunks.

You'll find large red maples scattered on both sides of the tunnel-like trail. The multiple trunks on these old trees indicate that they were cut decades ago and grew new trunks to survive. And just a few hundred feet from the sand pit on the swamp-side trail on the right is a large cluster of sensitive fern. Actually a small woody shrub and not a fern at all, it is sensitive to the cold and shrivels during the first few cool nights of autumn. Growing to about two feet in height, the sensitive fern can also be identified by its large wavy leaflets.

From the high ground reached by a dead-end right turn along the swamp trail, you should be able to spot the meandering border of the low-lying wetland, defined by an abrupt edge-line of trees. And on the Almanac Pond Road part of this loop, you'll discover a tall hill (tall is a relative term on Nantucket) which, on a clear day when the leaves are off the trees and shrubs, will afford you a view of Sesachacha Pond to the east with the ocean just beyond. To the southeast, you can glimpse Sankaty Head Lighthouse;

further south is the village of Siasconset, with more ocean views beyond. Turn to the north, and you can just see Great Point and Nantucket Sound.

When to Go

When you're looking for a change from watching sea life and walking Nantucket's shores, you can do what the woodland and freshwater wildlife seem to do when the island swells with summer people: disappear into the brush of Nantucket's moors.

Hearing the rufous-sided towee is easy spring through late summer, but heading out to Windswept Cranberry Bog to explore this loop through the bogs and moors is a treat no matter when you go. You'll catch only glimpses of Stump Pond and its swamp from the trails along its edges during spring and summer, but spectacular views abound in fall and winter when the leaves are off the trees.

Also, during winter, spring, and fall, you may enjoy trying to discern the various types of trees from each other. See how many different colors of spring buds there are and when each blossoms into a leaf. Walk out to the swamp's edge in the winter and check out the shapes, height, and density of the trees. For instance, on the longer loop just after entering the forest trail along the eastern shore of the pond, look for a straight-trunked stand of tupelo to the west which stands out, along with a few tall red maples nearby. And in the fall, the red leaves of the highbush blueberry will stand out. Right where the trail of this longer loop comes closest to the water, huckleberry, common in the moors, can be identified by its low, red leaves.

In spring and summer, you'll definitely want to use bug repellent. When there's sufficient snow on the ground, the bogs and this walk make for great cross-country skiing. Any time of year, if you'd like to bring children

larger than the sort you can carry on your back, be sure they will be able to walk two or three miles.

The bogs are beautiful during snowstorms and during the spring when all the plants and trees are budding, flowering, and sprouting their leaves. However, you'll likely find that you'll enjoy this walk a whole lot more if you go in late September through the end of October during the cranberry harvest (if it's happening). It's cool then, with no bugs, and the trails are easier to find, as are ripe wild grapes.

Best of all, though, when the bogs are active, it's a real treat to watch the harvest. Since these bogs are open to the public, you have the privilege of enjoying them all year long, even during the cranberry harvest. But remember to let the harvesters do their jobs, and do not, under any circumstances, walk down off the dikes into the bogs themselves or allow your dogs to go swimming in them. The bogs are full of cold water during the harvest in fall, and throughout the winter, and mucky mud in the warmer months. The cranberry plants themselves are also fragile and cannot support heavy foot traffic more than once a year.

As with so many of these walks, you'll miss out if you don't try these every season.

The Walks

Stump Pond Loop

Length: 2.5 Miles
Difficulty Rating: ***
Dogs: Yes
Children: Yes

Like the longer Stump Swamp–Almanac Pond loop, this walk begins on the dirt road leading into the Windswept Cranberry Bog. This road will open up into the bogs and continue toward a small, shingled utility shed. About 100 yards before the shed, take the first right.

Heed the signs that warn of honeybees. Cranberry growers, which lease the bogs from the Nantucket Conservation Foundation, use the bees to pollinate the flowers of its cranberry plants. Since wild honeybees, too, may seek out the pollen in the cranberry flowers, it's a good idea to allow the bees their space. Left alone, the bees will go about their age-old business and you can enjoy your walk.

Continue along the path toward a thick stand of maples, oaks, black tupelos, and hemlocks. After crossing over a culvert, turn left, keeping the trees on your right and the shed on your far left. Follow this dike as it snakes between bog and forest, eventually turning southwest. When you reach a fork, take the left that runs along a dike, keeping the shed in sight on your left across the bog.

As the shed slowly falls behind a stand of low trees shielding the remains of an old foundation (this is where the beehives are) and forming an island in the bogs, you'll see an intersection with a pond before it. When you can no longer see the shed behind the trees, veer right at the pond, keeping it on your left and heading south down a grassy road.

You'll notice that the pond is higher in elevation than the bogs. At harvest time, the cranberry growers open the channel between the pond and the bogs, flooding them with water. The buoyant ripe cranberries float to the surface, and crews skim them off the surface.

At the end of the grassy road is Stump Pond. From water's edge, follow a narrow trail west along the shore into the woods. When you reach a three-way split, choose the path that hugs the water. At one point, the path will take a jog into the woods, but it will quickly return to the pond. (If you don't want the pond experience, either of the other two trails will lead you back to the main trail.)

First leaving the edge of the pond and then returning, the shoreline path gradually rises and then falls toward a fat old oak tree. The trail continues to skirt the pond and is best navigated in the fall when the undergrowth abates and leaves are on the ground. The path will drop down below a dike

that circles around a small cove and then pop up again. About 50 feet from an old maple tree sitting just off shore in the muddy water southeast of the trail, look for a right turn to the west.

When the leaves are on the trees and bushes, this path can seem little more than a deer trail, so be careful and refer to the map often. The trail snakes through the brush, with swamp and sphagnum moss below to your right (north), and black tupelo trees ahead and to the left. When the trail opens into a small clearing with thigh-high ferns, look for a maple with a large burl on its trunk and turn right, keeping the maple on your right. This trail will lead you to Almanac Pond Road. You'll know you're on the right trail if, when you reach the road, you see on your left a large, fat oak with many limbs reaching skyward like tentacles. Turn right (north) onto this dirt way and follow it, past two farms and a bog, out onto the Polpis Road bike path. Turn right and follow the path about a quarter of a mile to reach the grass parking lot.

Alternatively, if you'd prefer to see more of the bogs on your return, you can re-enter the bogs off Almanac Pond Road just past the cobblestone entrance to a private residence on the east side of the road. Follow the dike along the bog until you see the utility shed and regain your bearings.

Stump Swamp—Almanac Pond Loop

Length: 2.9 Miles
Difficulty Rating: ****
Dogs: Yes
Children: Yes

Walk south into the bogs through a small stand of trees just south of the dirt and grass parking lot. To find your way across the bogs and into the woods, you will definitely find the map a helpful supplement to these directions.

Once through the trees and out in the open, you will see a shingled maintenance shed come into view. Walk toward it and keep it on your right. Take care to stay on the dirt road and not to take any roads that are more grass than dirt.

In late spring or early summer, you may see honeybees flying back and forth from their hives in an old foundation just past the shed. Walk quietly past them and they won't bother you. Their sole mission in spring is to haul pollen from the cranberry flowers back to their hives and thus unknowingly to pollinate the cranberry bushes. They're not interested in you unless you disturb them. Due to a glut in the supply of cranberries in the late 1990s through 2002, the former cranberry grower was forced to end its lease with the Nantucket Conservation Foundation and stopped harvesting Nantucket's cranberries, but the foundation operates part of the Bogs itself; however, walkers should continue to be wary of the bees.

Beyond the beehives, several houses and a barn will come into view, as will a faint split in the road. At the fork, go right and keep the houses and the barn on your left, heading toward an opening up a rise. A bog will be on your left between the dirt road and the buildings. You'll know you've gone the right way if, once through the opening, you spy a sandpit on your left. If you don't, refer to the map to recover your bearings.

Walk past the sandpit filled with piles of chaff left over from the fall cranberry harvest and head into the woods. The trail you're on now snakes past the swampy part of Stump Pond, a refuge for waterfowl and red-winged blackbirds. The views of the pond will lessen as the trail gradually turns away from the swamp side of the pond. Once the pond is completely out of sight and you're heading roughly southeast, you'll come to a proper right turn into the Nantucket bush. It's a dead end, but it's worth following for another view of the upper reaches of the pond and swamp system and the surrounding forest.

When you're all done looking at Stump Swamp, retrace your steps back to the main trail. Once you reach it, take a right and walk southeast. As the trail continues to arc to the east, a canopy of three large red maples comes into view on your left. Their roots are likely to be in moist soil or a wetland but remain hidden from view by a dense thicket. Depending on the season, you'll have a commanding view of three birds' nests atop these three maples.

Still running east, the trail will soon deposit you into a sandy intersection in the shape of an X. Cross the intersection diagonally, roughly southeast, referring to the map just to be sure, and follow the road that twists away to the south. When this road meets another, turn right; then, at a fork in the road, turn right again. After about 15 or 20 minutes of walking, just before this new road runs into another, take a hard right headed back north and ignore the left turn that appears minutes later. You're now on Almanac Pond Road. Refer to the map at this junction if you are uncertain.

Almanac Pond Road will slowly begin to rise in elevation toward a relatively tall hill. Find this nub of a bald spot when a sharp left turn presents itself. After taking in the views of Nantucket's eastern end, walk back down the hill the way you came, and continue north on Almanac Pond Road. You'll soon pass the shallow, periodically dry Almanac Pond—so named by early farmers who used the pond to predict the weather. Known technically as a wet meadow, the pond fills up with water in the spring and gradually dries out over the summer. It refills slightly in fall and can even have ice on it in winter. It can also spend the colder months completely dry.

Stay on road and ignore the left turn immediately after the pond. From there, it's a straight shot to Polpis Road. When you reach Polpis Road, turn right onto the bike path and follow it to the parking lot.

Getting There

On the south side of Polpis Road, just after the turn for Wauwinet Road coming from Milestone Road and just after the turn for Quidnet Road coming from Siasconset, is Windswept Cranberry Bog. It's marked by a maroon sign with white letters.

Polpis Road bike path passes right by this bog and its parking area. NRTA's 'Sconset via Polpis Road bus stops at Quidnet Road, so you can walk along the bike path to reach the parking area. Windswept Cranberry Bog is on your right.

Windswept Cranberry Bog

Map labels:

- QUIDNET RD.
- POLPIS ROAD
- PARKING / START
- BOGS
- ALMANACK POND ROAD
- STUMP POND
- (HILL)
- BARNARD
- N
- 0 .25

Neighborhoods

*To walk in the quiet lanes in the early
morning is to become part of the richness of historic Nantucket,
to enjoy an interwoven fabric of townscape, of street and land,
rather than of individual buildings.*
— Clay Lancaster, The Architecture of Historic Nantucket

189 + **Lily Pond-Grove Lane**

195 + **Siasconset Bluff**

201 + **Squam Pond**

207 + **Steps Beach**

Lily Pond-Grove Lane

Difficulty Rating: *
Dogs: Yes
Children: Yes

2.3 miles

The Area

Before automobiles first came to the island in May of 1900, the popular modes of transportation were riding animals, driving animals, and walking. Nantucket's first motorized vehicle, a Stanley Steamer, was driven by Arthur H. Folger, and while organically powered transportation was the preferred method of movement on the island for hundreds of years, Folger's "locomobile" eventually won out as the most popular form of conveyance on the Grey Lady.

This walk, which will guide you through the island's urban zone, into its suburbs, and out into the countryside, where you'll walk by the remnants of Nantucket's agrarian past, offers a unique trip down two of the routes many nineteenth-century islanders likely used to get into town.

What You'll See

The Lily Pond is mostly grown in with cattails and other aquatic plants. In the 1600s, a channel connected Lily Pond to Nantucket Harbor. As the island population grew—most people choosing to live in town—marshes and tidelands were filled to build houses and commercial buildings.

As you walk into this public sanctuary, you'll be treated to wonderful views of the western boundaries of town, including the lofty First Congregational Church on Center Street's Beacon Hill to the east. At the far northeastern end of the property, you'll find towering bulrushes, and tall trees opposite the rushes covered in a lush coat of ivy. Further out of town, at the intersection of Grove Lane (or Brush Hill Lane) and New Lane, you'll discover Nantucket's version of a town park, along with a graveyard. Just south of the intersection, from the top of a small rise topped by an apple tree, you'll get a view of the west side of town—an even better view in winter when the leaves are off the trees.

On the other side of the intersection, just north of where Grove Lane crosses New Lane, you can explore a graveyard on both sides of New Lane. A white sign on the west side reads, "The Old North originally the Gardner Burying Ground. Last resting place of Robert Inot, the first captain of the *Savannah*, the first steamship to cross the Atlantic, 1819." You may wish to allow extra time to explore this historical graveyard.

When to Go

Enjoy this walk in spring for the apple trees that bloom along the path and the swarms of red-winged blackbirds. Return in August for the ripe blackberries dangling from their bushes. (Don't forget a good plastic container!)

Fall is a great time to take this walk, when you can enjoy the colorful leaves of the hardwood trees that ring the Lily Pond. And walking this route in winter, especially with a fresh coating of snow on the land and buildings, should be part of everyone's Nantucket Experience.

The Walk

The walk begins in the center of town on Academy Hill. The Academy Hill Apartments are dedicated to some of the island's elderly citizens. The giant brick building was originally the private Academy Hill School (circa 1800), where island children were educated well into the 1960s. Walk to the left (south) of the building and find a set of stairs that lead west down and away from the building and onto a narrow way that opens onto Lily Street.

Cross Lily Street and walk down the Land Bank's grass path between the two houses directly across the street. You've just entered the Land Bank's Lily Pond property.

Walk down into a meadow that is frequently moist through the year and sometimes under several inches of water during the spring. At the end of the meadow, a worn plank leads to a boardwalk that the Land Bank installed in the summer of 1998. The boardwalk extends into the heart of the Lily Pond parcel. When it ends, turn right and take your time exploring the mowed lawns and paths around the Lily Pond.

When you've finished exploring the Lily Pond land, return to the end of the boardwalk but walk past it, keeping it on your left while walking west to the road ahead, North Liberty Street. Once on the street, turn right (north) and walk about 50 feet, then turn left onto Brush Hill Lane. Walk up this gradually narrowing street until you come to a crossroad called New Lane. On your left is a green Land Bank post marking the in-town open space. If you have time, walk left (southeast) up onto the field.

Once you've explored the graveyard and the Land Bank's meadow, return to the green Land Bank marker, cross New Lane, and continue west on Grove Lane. Past several houses on both sides, the right side of the road will gently narrow to a wide path. On the right is the Abbott Johnson Wildlife Preserve, packed with the same cattails that ring No Bottom Pond just to the north. You should be able to see the pond in late fall and winter, but heavy growth will hide it in spring and summer. You are now walking in the northernmost part of the Hummock Pond watershed. Water from Grove Lane flows south, via ditches and groundwater, to replenish Hummock Pond's water levels.

On the south side of Grove Lane are two farms with fields in which several horses and ponies munch on grass and other vegetation. Continue on Grove Lane, and it will eventually connect with Crooked Lane. From this intersection, you can retrace your steps back to town, or you can turn left onto Crooked Lane, cross Madaket Road, and walk back to town (east) via the Madaket Road bike path. Madaket Road was one of the routes into town from the western end of the island. When you reach the beginning of Madaket Road, walk straight past Caton Circle on your left.

You're walking along the very top of Main Street. Stay on this street as the asphalt turns to paving blocks and then to the cobblestones that legend holds were originally fieldstones used as ballast in seafaring ships. To return to the start of the walk, follow Main Street until you reach its intersection with Centre Street, turn left, and walk to the intersection of Centre with Broad. If you wish, a left-turn onto Gay or Quince Street will return you to Academy Hill.

Getting There

To reach Academy Hill and the start of the walk, take either Gay Street west from the top of Broad Street or Quince Street west from Centre Street in town to where they terminate at the top of the hill. In summer, if you cannot avoid driving into town, you will find that parking is more plentiful on the streets leading into and out of town, including Union, Orange, Upper Main, Easton, North Water, Fair, and Washington Streets, as well as in the town's parking lot on Washington Street. To avoid the hassle of summer parking, you can ride downtown on any of the NRTA shuttles. Or, since bicycles are much easier to park than cars, you can cycle into town and lock your bike to any of the racks on Federal Street next to the Visitor Center, at the intersection of Federal and Main streets across from the Hub, at the Steamship Authority terminal, or at the Grand Union.

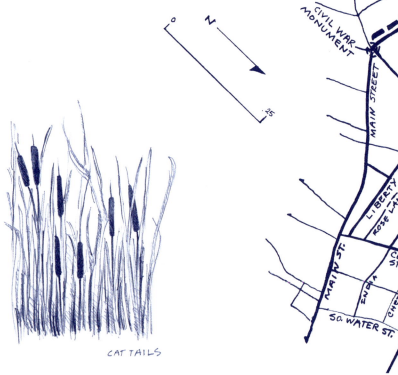

CAT TAILS

Siasconset Bluff

Difficulty Rating: *
Dogs: Yes
Children: Yes

2.4 miles

The Area

Were it not for the benevolent and perceptive William Flagg, a significant stretch of the bluff in Siasconset would be inaccessible to the general public. True, the bluff from the top of North Gully Road south to the wooden bridge over Gully Road would always offer public views of the sea—from a distance—but a traditionally public section of the bluff would be closed off.

Hail William Flagg, who gave most of *his* bluff—Flagg named it Sankaty Heights after he divided it up into 88 lots—to the Town of Nantucket, along with the dunes and beach in front of his bluff. What remains of Flagg's generous donation is a path that snakes along the bluff across the lawns of the owners of some of the best ocean views in the world. That's right: past privet hedges clipped into the shapes of whales spouting water, across finely coifed lawns, around shrubs, and all with the vast expanse of the Atlantic Ocean literally a stone's throw away.

The walk used to terminate at the Sankaty Head Lighthouse, but in the last ten years, extensive bluff erosion forced several property owners near the end of Baxter Road to move their houses inland, and that part of the walk tumbled down the bluff.

What You'll See

The ocean. More ocean than you've seen without flying over it or being shipwrecked on it. The entire route you'll walk offers breath-taking views of the Atlantic Ocean. If you're really really lucky, you'll see right whales September through November, but mostly you'll see northern gannets skimming the waves then diving for fish, and 12 varieties of gulls in the winter. During the summer, all manner of inland birds haunt the path along the bluff including, but not limited to, cat birds, robins, Carolina Wrens, Baltimore orioles, purple and gold finches, grackles, cardinals, blue jays, brown-headed cowbirds, crows, red-winged blackbirds, and song sparrows.

When to Go

To be fair to those who own land and houses along Baxter Road, this walk is to be treated sensitively. While anyone can traverse the seaward edge of these lawns, it can be a little uncomfortable walking across a lawn that doesn't belong to you while the owners are present. So the perfect time, then, is late fall through early spring, when ninety-nine percent of these seasonal bluff dwellers are back in "America."

A few of the houses are occupied year-round, but their owners are hip to the timeless generosity of Flagg's gift and the people who enjoy it as an off-season stroll. But if you feel like it, a stroll along this bluff path on an early summer evening or morning is worth the effort for the changing hues of ocean and sky. Any time of day is good, but try a late autumn afternoon leading into sunset so you can catch the colors on the water while your shoes rustle through the leaves.

During the winter, twelve varieties of gulls make Nantucket their off-season home, and most of them can be seen feeding just offshore in the chilly surf among seals and northern gannets diving for fish. Bring a pair of binoculars to spot these marine animals. The binoculars might also come in handy in springtime, when endangered right whales can sometimes be seen breaching well offshore on their way north.

The Walk

The 'Sconset Bluff Walk begins in the village of Siasconset on Front Street at the start of Broadway, a one-way street that runs parallel to the ocean north to south. The narrow, white pebbled alley runs along the bluff from a house, marked with a quarterboard that reads "Casa Marina," adjacent the 'Sconset Market.

On Front Street, keep an eye out for the second hard right, an ancient, narrow asphalt side street between two houses that heads down the bluff. This unmarked road is North Gully Road, which, followed all the way down the bluff to its sea level end, deposits you in Codfish Park.

Avoid this detour by turning left onto the first lawn you come to, at a sign marking the start of the bluff section of this walk, and following the path through a hedge. The path generally traces the bluff edges of the lawns and breaks through privet hedges, but it occasionally wanders closer to the houses on some of the lawns. Stick to the path, which is worn well down to dirt across each lawn; the home owners, while tolerant of light foot traffic, would rather not see the path widen nor have its users explore their properties.

Public access along the bluff ends after you encounter a sign reading: "Walk ends 700 feet, return here to exit." While the sign estimates 700 feet, the actual amount is probably around 400 or 500 feet, because erosion of the bluff has whittled away more of the path every year. After exploring the last few hundred feet of the bluff walk, return to the sign and then walk back along the bluff to the village of Siasconset. There. You're walking in Flagg's footsteps.

Getting There

Travel to Siasconset Village by either Milestone Road or Polpis Road. Both of these have bike paths that originate from rotary at the confluence of Orange Street, Sparks Avenue, Old South Road, and Milestone Road. In season, two NRTA bus routes from town lead to Siasconset. Refer to the seasonal NRTA bus schedule for bus stops and times.

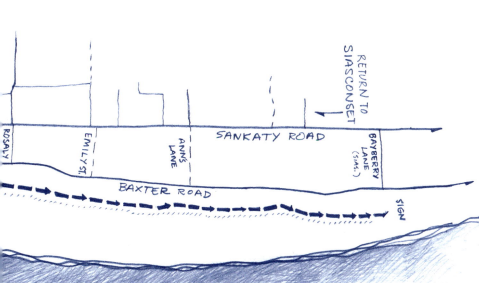

2.4 miles

Difficulty Rating: **
Dogs: Yes
Children: Yes

The Area

Ponder the catbird. It is your basic, robin-size bird with nothing more than a black-capped head to break up the monotony of its gray body. Ever opportunists, these talkative, warm-weather migrants descend on Nantucket each spring to do more than just mate. One of their missions seems to be bilking the unwary summer renter out of whole loaves of bread, crackers, and even salt-and-vinegar potato chips. They're polite scavengers that appear almost tame, gaunt, and migration-weary—a ploy they engage to endear doting admirers.

To appreciate fully this slate-colored scavenger that winters as far south as Central America, you must be in its element—which is all of Nantucket's underbrush. My own favorite spot is anywhere along Squam Road and around Squam Pond, where thickets of raspberry, beach rose, wild grapes and low scrub oak make perfect cover for the vocal catbird. In fact, one bird hidden in this dense Nantucket tangle can give the impression that a dozen are carrying on an avian conversation like a chattering flock of jays or a cawing murder of crows. And the catbird call really does sound like a cat's meow, combined with an exhausting repertoire of other peeps, chirps, and tweets that make it tough to believe you're listening to just one type of bird.

Nantucket's eastern shores are some of the least populated parts of the island. Walkers (and catbirds) who venture anywhere from Great Point down to Tom Nevers Head can find solitude at almost any time of year.

Squam Road, which runs between Wauwinet and Quidnet, is a perfect place to concentrate on the natural sounds of Nantucket's wilderness.

What You'll See

Take your time to listen for the catbirds as you walk along Squam Road. Also, watch for the barn, bank, and tree swallows performing their aerial ballet in search of bugs.

When you walk down the beach path off Squam Road, keep your eyes open for a view of the Squam Pond—a kettle hole created when a giant block of ice left by the glacier melted during the Wisconsin Era, 15,000 years ago. The pond attracts ducks, gulls, several varieties of herons, and, of course the omnipresent red-winged blackbird. In warm weather, be prepared for the smaller flying and biting bugs that all moist inland areas nurture.

Once you're on the beach, the rest is up to you. If you're a fan of folklore, walk about a half-mile north and you'll be at Squam Head. In Algonquian, the name of this spot, *Wanashquiompskut*, means "at the top of the rock."

Legend has it that a family by the name of Bunker buried its nest egg of gold near their house at Squam Head. After a band of French pirates burgled the Bunker home and kidnapped Captain Bunker in 1695, they forced him to guide their ship through Nantucket and Vineyard sounds to Tarpaulin Cove. Bunker managed to escape, but the whole ordeal rattled him so much that he forgot where he buried the family fortune. For years, he and his kin dug holes around their homestead in search of the gold but never found it.

For those with angling on their minds, however, there is fishing gold in this area. Bluefish and striped bass can be caught spring through fall, three hours before and three hours after low tide all along Nantucket's ocean shores.

When to Go

The relative peace and quiet of Squam Road makes this a good walk any time of the year. In the warmer months, you are rewarded by the smell of beach roses and the opportunity to cool your tired, hot feet once you've reached the water. Spring and summer are also fantastic for sunrises, and on the night of a full moon, the big orange disk rising out of the ocean makes this an easy sell at dusk. In winter, you can't beat the sunsets, because there's usually a half sky of clouds waiting to be painted by the sun's fading rays.

In late summer and early fall, I bring all the containers I can carry so I can pick the wild grapes. Their vines grow all along Squam Road, nearly suffocating the bushes and trees that support them.

The Walk

The walk begins at the gatehouse and parking area owned by the Nantucket Conservation Foundation and staffed by the Trustees of Reservations, near the end of Wauwinet Road and just before the Wauwinet Inn. From the parking area, walk out to Wauwinet Road and turn left, walking southwest past the air hoses on the north side of the road and down to the next left, Squam Road. Follow Squam Road beyond the 17th telephone pole to between houses #55 and #49 on the ocean side of this dirt road.

You're headed for a strip of beach accessed by a narrow public way between two private properties. A short distance after the 17th pole, the road heads downhill. Just before a large gate on the ocean side of the road, find the grassy trail blocked by two boulders meant to keep vehicles out. Turn left onto the trail and continue on to the beach.

This walk has no loop, so to return, simply walk back the way you came.

Getting There

Don't expect to shorten the walk by skipping the stroll down Squam Road and driving to the public way. Because the dirt road is so narrow and the brush so thick and overgrown, there is no room to park anywhere along this section of the road.

Traveling from town by car or by bicycle, turn from Polpis Road onto Wauwinet Road and follow it until you reach the Nantucket Conservation

Foundation's red-trimmed gatehouse, adjacent to a dirt parking area. You can park on the right side of the parking area. NRTA bus riders have a long walk to reach the gatehouse, because the 'Sconset via Polpis bus stops at the start of Wauwinet Road.

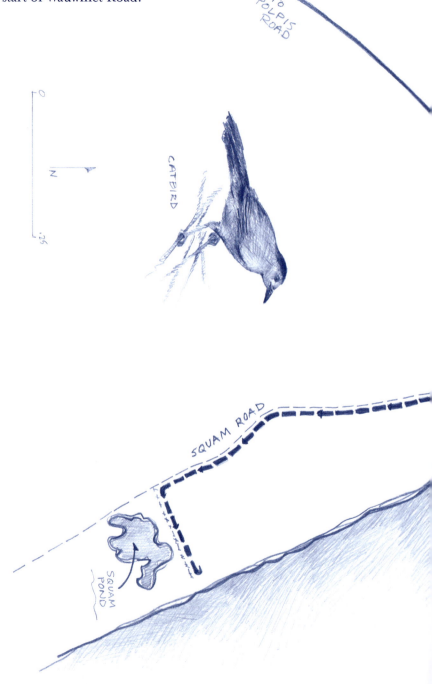

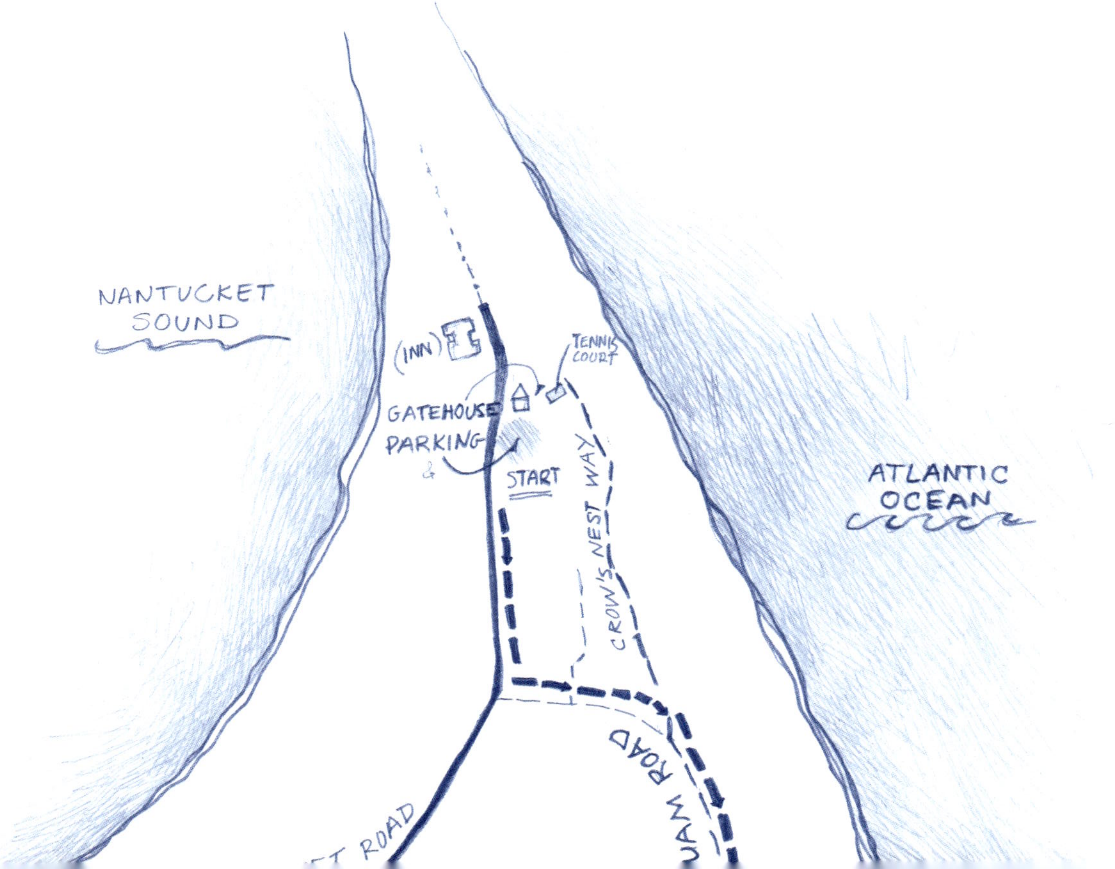

NANTUCKET SOUND

T ROAD

GATEHOUSE PARKING

(INN)

START

TENNIS COURT

CROW'S NEST WAY

UAM ROAD

ATLANTIC OCEAN

205 • WALKING NANTUCKET • SQUAM POND

Steps Beach

Short Loop

Length: 2 Miles
Difficulty Rating: **
Dogs: Yes
Children: Yes

Town Loop

Length: .5 miles; 3.1 miles RT from Broad Street
Difficulty Rating: *
Dogs: No
Children: Yes

The Area

Steps Beach, at the foot of what Nantucketers call "The Cliff," is on the island's north shore and overlooks Nantucket Harbor and Nantucket Sound. Imposing summer houses on the bluff above, a gull's-eye-view of the island's main boat thoroughfare, and the delightfully warm waters of Nantucket Sound make this the wrong place to walk when the island is full.

However, on a hot, sticky summer evening, the ocean air is not usually enough to cool one down for the night. So when you can't take the heat, get over to Lincoln Avenue, walk down the 41 steps that give the beach its name, and go for a late night dip in Nantucket Sound. The Sound is warmer than the ocean and, most nights, just a little cooler than the air.

Though busy, the beach is also great during summer days and late afternoons, and for people, and their children who want a tamer spot for swimming.

The Jetties Beach part of this walk is also ideal for children and their parents, because it is much larger than Steps Beach and has bathrooms nearby, as well as a concession stand, swings, and a jungle gym.

What You'll See

When you see the view from the top of bluff overlooking Steps Beach, you'll understand why Cliff dwellers spent several million dollars for their summer "cottages." To the west, the sun sets behind splendid views of the North Shore and Tuckernuck and Muskeget islands. To the northeast, you can see Great Point Lighthouse at the head of a low, thin ribbon of sand that extends southeast to Coskata woods, Coatue, and the harbor.

Down on Steps Beach and over at Jetties Beach, shell collectors will discover a lifetime supply of slipper shells. Sometimes these pinkish shells cover the beach like the cobblestones on Main Street. Slipper shells are a favorite of gulls, which seem to delight in plucking them out of the shallow water just off shore, eating their contents, and discarding the empty shells to wash up on the beach like tiny lost shoes.

In addition to the slipper shells, you may find yourself trudging through mountains of dead eelgrass blown and washed ashore by heavy seas. This might be a deterrent to some, but for most beach lovers, it's a whole other plane of beachcombing. The stringy green harbor weed traps sea treasures, along with other flotsam and jetsam, as it rolls up on the beach and dries to black and brown.

If you chose a night swim at Steps Beach, you'll take comfort that Nantucket Sound is safer for swimming than the surf on the South

Shore—you're not likely to see the waves crashing on the beach, and into you. The other special reason to swim here at night is for a natural underwater light show that Nantucketers call "the phosphorescence."

According the Woods Hole Oceanographic Institute, the cause of this phenomenon is a species of otherwise clear jellyfish called Leidy's Comb Jelly, which is at its most plentiful in the waters around Nantucket and Cape Cod from mid-August through late September. This lemon-size oval jellyfish, classified as a species of plankton, is nearly invisible in the sea during the day and impossible to see at night, unless you are there to make it light up. By stirring up the water with your hands, wading, and basically splashing around, you'll agitate these jellyfish, causing them to light up in a bright greenish blue.

During the day, minnows dart all along the shallows near the shore, and moon shell snails, whelks and knobbed whelks, and horseshoe crabs all move along in knee to ankle-deep water. Herring, black-backed, and laughing gulls hunt for this shelled food, along with the cormorants that dive for fish. Starfish and sand dollars have been known to wash up occasionally.

Out at Jetties Beach, you'll find all of the above, plus the best view you can get without a boat, of Nantucket Sound and all the boat activity traveling in and out of the harbor.

If it's low tide, you can explore around the edges of the west jetty. For obvious safety and liability reasons, heed the warning sign near the first rocks and *don't* hike out onto the jetty. The jetty's slippery, uneven boulders are dangerous even when the sea and wind are calm. However, the jetty area is a great place to fish and to watch the sunset.

When to Go

During the summer, don't miss the chance to swim at Steps Beach at night, or during the day. The shallower, calmer waters of the north shore make this an ideal beach for young children. However, expect a lot of people during the summer days because of the beach's easy access. Autumn, winter, spring are equally enjoyable down on the beach minus the swimming option, so adding Jetties Beach and Brant Point to your explorations makes an off-season walk more enjoyable.

The Walk

You can start this walk in town or up on Lincoln Avenue. Just off Cliff Road, Lincoln Avenue is an oval-shaped road ringed with split rail fencing around a grassy common. On the waterside of the informal parking area at the west end of Lincoln Avenue, a short path leads to the top of the Steps Beach stairs. Descend the stairs and walk through the dunes and down onto the beach for a swim, or a picnic on non-swimming days. But do not walk far in either direction—this public beach's bordering properties are privately owned.

When you're ready to move on, ascend the stairs and go left (southeast) onto Lincoln Avenue. Follow this road until the next left, a cobblestone lane called Cobblestone Hill. Walk down this street and turn right onto North Beach Street. Walking southeast in the general direction of town, take the next left, Bathing Beach Road, and head for the water.

If walking from town is your thing, begin at the start of Cliff Road at the intersection of Easton and North Water streets, opposite the Captain Gardner House. Walk up along Cliff Road, past the guesthouses on either side, take a right onto Mooer's Avenue, and then turn left onto Lincoln Avenue.

On the return, when you've exited the beach parking lot onto Bathing Beach Road, either find your way back up Cobblestone Hill to your transportation, or stroll back to town by way of Hulbert Avenue, the first left before North Beach Street as you walk away from the beach. This is a great way to make a loop out of this walk and to see some of the larger homes on the harbor. Walk to the end of Hulbert Avenue and turn left on Easton Street. A short walk to Easton's harbor end will deposit you on Brant Point. From there, walk west on Easton Street to its intersection with North Beach Street and turn left to find your way back to town.

You can also walk from the Jetties Beach parking lot out to the end of Bathing Beach Road, turn left (south) onto North Beach Street, and follow this road back into town.

Getting There

Take Mooer's Avenue off Cliff Road to the northwestern end of Lincoln Avenue. At the end of Mooer's Avenue, turn left onto Lincoln Avenue. NRTA's Madaket bus stops at the intersection of Cliff Road and North Liberty Street. Mooer's Avenue is just west of North Liberty Street on the north side of Cliff Road. Cyclists can follow the same directions by biking from town to Cliff Road.

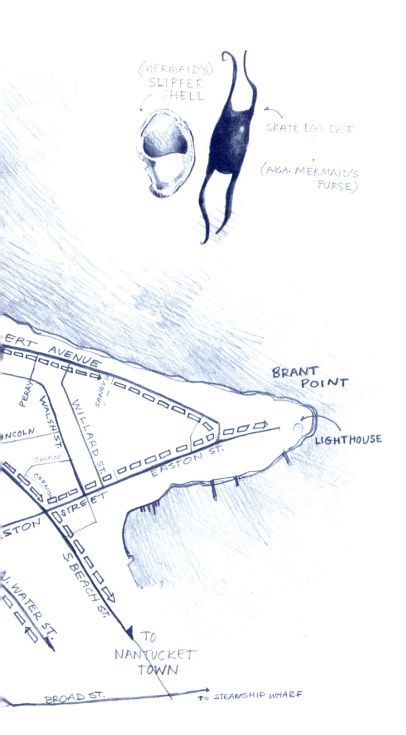

Algonquian — A family of languages formerly spoken by Native Americans in an area extending from Labrador westward to the Rocky Mountains, west-southwestward through Michigan and Illinois, and southwestward along the Atlantic Coast to Cape Hatteras, including tribes of Arapaho, Blackfoot, Cheyenne, Cree, Fox, Massachusett, Micmac, Ojibwa, and Powhatan

Anadromous — Fish species that spawn in freshwater ponds, lakes, rivers, streams, and estuaries, but live in saltwater ecosystems

Autumnal Equinox — The time of year when the sun crosses the plane of the earth's equator, making night and day of approximately equal length all over the earth; occurs around September 22, signaling the start of fall

Barrier Beach — A narrow, low-lying strip of beach and dune that exists parallel to an island or the mainland as either a peninsula or a small island just offshore; acts as a natural wave break, protecting coastal areas from the ravages of open ocean wave and storms, and provides habitat for nesting shore birds and other animals; often protects salt marshes as well

The Bluff — Overlooking the Atlantic Ocean from the village of Siasconset on the eastern end of Nantucket, a cliff of clay, dirt, and sand that runs from just north of the Sankaty Head Lighthouse to the south end of Codfish Park at Gully Road

Brackish — Water that is slightly salty, resulting from a mixture of fresh and saltwater

Burl — A woody outgrowth on a tree that is typically spherical and harder than the main wood growth of the tree

Catadromous — Fish species that spawn in the ocean but spend their lives predominantly in freshwater ecosystems

The Cliff — A section of Nantucket Town off the northeast side of Cliff Road, featuring large summer homes perched on a low cliff overlooking Steps and Jetties Beaches and Nantucket Sound

Coastal Heathland — Called "moors" by Nantucketers, an undulating landscape on Nantucket between Milestone and Polpis Roads at the northern end of the island, marking the deposits of sand and rock from the farthest reach of the island-forming glacier's southern edges; contains many of the plants found in sandplain grasslands.

Coastal Plain — A plain extending along a coastline

Ecosystem — A localized group of interdependent organisms together with the environment that they inhabit and on which they depend

Endangered Species — Any species of plant or animal threatened by extinction

Estuarine — A plant or animal found in an estuary, the seaward part of a river or stream in which the river's current meets the sea's tide

Exclosure — A wire mesh cage placed over endangered shore birds' nests to protect the birds, their eggs, and their young from predators

First Bridge and Second Bridge — Nantucketers' names for the two successive culverts — the first bisecting the north and south ends of Long Pond and the second connecting Hither Creek with Long Pond — on the Madaket Road just west of the last entrance to the landfill

Fledging — The process by which birds raise their young from the time they hatch until they fly

Head of the Harbor — The upper reaches of Nantucket Harbor, bordered by Wauwinet, Coskata Pond and its woods, Pocomo Point, and Coatue from Bass Point east

Heathland — A tract of open and uncultivated land supporting plants and animals that are salt-spray tolerant and have poor soils

Hillock — A small hill or foothill

Hummock — A tract of land elevated above the general level of a marshy region

Intertidal Zone — The part of the shore, between the low tide mark and the high tide mark, where marine life is sustained by the ebb and flow of the tides

Jetty — A structure of large rocks forming a pier, or piles of rocks projecting into the sea or other body of water to protect a harbor from strong currents, tides, and ocean waves

Kettle Hole — A pond, such as Maxcy Pond, Almanac Pond, and the Pout Ponds, formed by a huge chunk of ice, left behind by the glacier, that pressed into the earth of Nantucket just beneath ground water level; with no streams flowing into or out of, kettle ponds are at the mercy of the atmosphere and must rely on ground water levels and rain to remain full

Littleneck — A smaller quahog usually shucked and served raw on the half shell.

Littoral Drift — The drifting (and depositing) of marine sediments, like sand, in patterns parallel to the contours of a beach, due to the action of waves and currents

Marine & Coastal Resources Department — Town agency responsible for monitoring and enforcing all activities on and in Nantucket's harbors, including the health of the island's harbors and ponds, shellfish propagation and harvesting, boat holding tank pump-out, the town pier, boat operator policing, search and rescue, public landings, harbormaster patrol, mooring field issues, and derelict boats

Moon Tide — A local phrase to describe the extremely high and low tides that occur during the period of a full moon

Northern Harrier — Formerly called the "marsh hawk": a threatened species of hawk in Massachusetts known for its ability to hover low over the scrub while searching for rodents; nests on the ground; lives and hunts in sandplain grasslands and low wooded areas on Nantucket, Martha's Vineyard, Block Island, and Long Island

Outwash Plain — A broad, sloping landform consisting of sand and gravel left behind by the glacier; e.g. within a mile inland of the ocean on Nantucket's South Shore

Overwash — Waves that break high on a beach, typically at high tide during a storm, and wash up over the dunes and inland properties

Raptor — A bird of prey that hunts during daylight hours; e.g. the American vulture, hawks, eagles, and falcons

Rip — A narrow, turbulent current flowing strongly from the shore to the sea, visible as a stream of agitated water, such as those present at Great Point, Smith's Point, Eel Point, Miacomet Beach, and Siasconset Beach

Sachem — The basic term for a North American Indian chief; also the description for the chief of a confederation of the Algonquian tribes of the North Atlantic coast

Salt Pond — A pond, usually located in close proximity to the ocean, with a low level of salinity that supports both freshwater and saltwater aquatic vegetation and animal life

Sandplain Grassland — Open habitats of predominantly grasses, low shrubs, and annual and perennial wild flowers, akin to Mid-western prairies, typically found on the south side of Nantucket; geologically known as outwash plains, on which glacial meltwaters left sand.

Schoolies — Fisherman's name for immature striped bass below the legal limit of 28 inches

Scrub Oak — An aggressive, low oak that thrives in dry, rocky soil and is characterized by scrubby growth and branches that extend outward as much as upward

Siasconset — Believed to mean "at the little muddy place" in Algonquian; the name for the easternmost village of Nantucket; sometimes abbreviated with an apostrophe as 'Sconset, although several island publications now ignore the apostrophe altogether

Slack Tide — A period of time between low and high tide, typically about 15 and 30 minutes, when no tidal current prevails

Stormwash — See Overwash

Vernal equinox — The time of year when the sun crosses the plane of the earth's equator, making night and day of approximately equal length all over the earth; occurs around March 21 and signals the start of spring

Wet meadow — Also called a "seasonal pond": a shallow depression that meets the water table during part of the year and collects rainwater, forming a temporary pond

Wisconsin Era — The fourth stage of the glaciation of North America during the Pleistocene Epoch

Wrack line — A line of flotsam and jetsam marking the reach of the strongest waves during the last high tide

Appendix

Nantucket's Land Conservation Groups

Nantucket Conservation Foundation

The Nantucket Conservation Foundation, the largest land conservation group on the island, was organized in 1963 and owns more than 8,700 acres. The NCF welcomes the public onto most of its properties. You'll know you've found their land when you spot a maroon concrete post displaying the Foundation's logo. The Foundation offices are at 118 Cliff Road (508-228-2884), and additional information is available at the Web site, *http://www.nantucketconservation.com*.

Nantucket Islands Land Bank

The first of its kind in the United States, the Nantucket Land Bank was founded in 1984 and owns more than 2,187 acres on Nantucket. While it welcomes donations of land, the Land Bank acquires most of its properties by two purchasing methods: a two-percent tax levied on property transfers finances much of the Land Bank's acquisitions, as do bonds taken out by the Town of Nantucket.

In addition to the land of the 18-hole Miacomet Golf Club, the Land Bank also owns considerable beach property and inland holdings that it allows the public to enjoy passively. The Land Bank's property marker is a wooden post capped with a green and white Land Bank designation.

The Nantucket Islands Land Bank is administered from 22 Broad Street (508-228-7240). Go to *http://www.nantucketlandbank.org* for the complete Land Bank story.

Nantucket Land Council

More a lobby for island environmental justice than a buyer of undeveloped land, the Nantucket Land Council works in concert with the other island land groups. The Land Council, which was incorporated in 1974, first clears title to a property and then passes the land on to the Land Bank, the Conservation Foundation, or another island land conservation organization, sometimes only for the cost of legal expenses. While the Council does own and maintain a few hundred acres around Nantucket, its staff spends a good percentage of its time at Conservation Commission, Planning Board, Planning Commission, Historic District Commission, and other town review board meetings, making sure new development and house plans don't encroach upon or destroy the island's natural world. The Land Council is a champion of the island's harbor watershed and groundwater supply, and it subsidizes rare species and water quality research. It also helps land owners place their property under conservation restrictions. These restrictions prohibit development on the land while preserving it in its natural state. As of this printing, the Land Council has negotiated conservation restriction for 33 parcels of land on more than 400 acres.

You will find the Nantucket Land Council on Ash Lane (508-228-2818) and at *http://www.nantucketlandcouncil.org*.

Massachusetts Audubon Society

About 900 of the 28,000 acres owned statewide by the Massachusetts Audubon Society are on Nantucket. Operating on membership dues, donations, and federal and private grants, the Massachusetts Audubon Society, founded in 1890, is separate from the National Audubon Society. The MAS watches over 37 wildlife sanctuaries in the state, including one at Hummock Pond and a second at Sesachacha Pond on Nantucket. These properties are marked by the Massachusetts Audubon Society's maroon and white signs. To learn more about the Society, log onto its Web site, *http://www.massaudubon.org*, or phone them at 508-228-9208.

The Trustees of Reservations

A steward of mostly sand dunes, beaches, and saltmarshes, the Trustees of Reservations owns and manages 1,117 acres of Nantucket's northeastern tip, called Great Point. The Trustees of Reservations is the oldest private statewide preservation and conservation organization and holds and manages more than 33,000 acres in Massachusetts. On Nantucket, the Trustees let four-wheel drivers onto their beaches for the annual sticker permit fee of $100 and $125 for non-residents. The walking public is welcomed at no charge. You'll know you're on Trustees land if you spot green and white plastic signs bearing the Trustees' insignia. For Nantucket information, call 508-228-3359, and to explore the rest of the Trustees' properties around the state, explore the Web page *http://www.thetrustees.org*.

The Nantucket Conservation Commission

A selectmen-appointed town board of seven members, enforces local and state wetlands bylaws laws on the island. The ConCom, local jargon for this wetland regulatory board, owns 108.7 acres of Nantucket. You can reach the Conservation Commission at 508-228-7230 and find them at 37 Washington St.

Madaket Land Trust and the 'Sconset Trust

Two smaller island groups, the Madaket Land Trust and the 'Sconset Trust, each own less than 100 acres on their respective ends of the island. They depend primarily on the generosity of private donors to fund purchases of land that will preserve the character, wildlife, and vegetation of their island villages.

You will reach the Madaket Land Trust (508-228-0841) only during the summer, since its members are all summer residents, but the 'Sconset Trust is accessible year-round at 508-228-9917.

Resources used in producing this book

Organizations:

The Nantucket Conservation Foundation, 118 Cliff Road, Nantucket, Massachusetts 02554

The Nantucket Islands Land Bank, 22 Broad Street, Nantucket, Massachusetts 02554

Books:

Alden, Peter, and Brian Cassie. *Field Guide to New England*. New York: Alfred A. Knopf, 1998.

Brenizer, Meredith Marshall. *Nantucket Indians — Legends and Accounts Before 1659*. Self-published. Reprinted on Nantucket: Mitchell's Book Corner, 1974.

Chamberlain, Barbara Blau. *These Fragile Outposts*. Garden City: Natural History Press, 1964.

Farrand, Jr., John. *Eastern Birds*. New York: McGraw Hill Book Company, 1988.

Gosner, Kenneth L. *Atlantic Seashore*. Boston: Houghton-Mifflin, 1978.

Green, Eugene, and William Sachse. *Names of the Land — Cape Cod, Nantucket, Martha's Vineyard, and the Elizabeth Islands — A Compendium of Cape Area Proper Names with Derivations*. Chester: The Globe Pequot Press, 1932.

Lamb, Jane. *Wauwinet*. Nantucket: Self-published 1990.

Lamb, Jane. *Wauwinet Unzipped*. Nantucket: Self-published 1994.

Oldale, Robert N. *Cape Cod, Martha's Vineyard, & Nantucket: The Geologic Story*. Yarmouth Port: On Cape Publications, 1992.

Marshall, Esther S. *Polpis Past and Present — Nantucket*. Waltham: Wells Bindery, April 1974.

Sibley, David Allen. *The Sibley Guide to Birds*. New York: The Chanticleer Press, 2000.